fish
food

bay books

fish
food

Contents

Starters

Fried whitebait

500 g (1 lb 2 oz) whitebait
2 teaspoons sea salt
2 tablespoons plain
 (all-purpose) flour
1½ tablespoons cornflour
 (cornstarch)
2 teaspoons finely chopped flat-leaf
 (Italian) parsley
vegetable oil, for deep-frying
lemon wedges, for serving

Combine the whitebait and sea salt in a bowl and mix well. Cover and refrigerate until needed.

Combine the sifted flours and parsley in a bowl and season well with freshly ground black pepper. Fill a deep-fat fryer or large saucepan one-third full of oil and heat to 180°C (350°F), or until a cube of white bread dropped into the oil browns in 15 seconds. Toss a third of the whitebait in the flour mixture, shake off the excess flour, and deep-fry for 1½ minutes, or until pale and crisp. Drain well on crumpled paper towels. Repeat with the remaining whitebait.

Just before serving, reheat the oil to 190°C (375°C), or until a cube of white bread browns in 10 seconds, and fry the whitebait a second time, in batches, for 1 minute each batch, or until lightly browned. Drain on crumpled paper towels, salt lightly (this will help absorb any excess oil) and serve while hot with some lemon wedges.

Serves 4

Grilled sardines with basil and lemon

1 lemon, cut into thin slices
8 whole sardines, gutted, scaled
  and cleaned
coarse sea salt
80 ml (⅓ cup) olive oil
3 tablespoons torn basil leaves or
  whole small leaves

Fish substitution
  small herring, mackerel

Preheat a griller (broiler) or griddle to very hot. Insert a couple of slices of lemon inside each sardine and season on both sides with the sea salt and some freshly ground black pepper. Drizzle them with half of the olive oil.

Put the sardines on a baking tray and grill (broil) for 3 minutes on each side or place the fish directly onto the griddle. Check to see if the fish are cooked by lifting the top side and checking the inside of the fish. The flesh should look opaque. Remove and place in a shallow serving dish. Scatter the basil over the sardines and drizzle with the remaining olive oil. Serve warm or at room temperature.

Serves 4

Cuban-style prawns with rum

100 ml (3½ fl oz) white rum
few drops of Tabasco sauce
zest and juice of a lime
2 teaspoons Worcestershire sauce
2½ tablespoons plain
  (all-purpose) flour
generous pinch of ground cumin
generous pinch of freshly grated
  nutmeg
24 tiger prawns (shrimp), peeled
  and deveined, tails intact
25 g (1 oz) butter
80 ml (⅓ cup) olive oil
4 large garlic cloves, crushed
1 tablespoon chopped parsley
1 tablespoon chopped coriander
  (cilantro) leaves

Fish substitution
  freshwater crayfish

Mix together the rum, Tabasco, lime zest and juice and Worcestershire sauce in a small bowl.

Mix the flour with the cumin and nutmeg and season with salt and freshly ground black pepper. Dip the prawns in the seasoned flour to lightly coat before cooking.

Melt half of the butter with half of the oil in a large sauté or frying pan and, when hot, add half of the garlic and half of the prawns. Cook for 4–5 minutes, or until the prawns have turned a pale pink colour and are lightly golden on the outside. Lift onto a serving plate and keep warm. Repeat with the remaining butter, oil, garlic and prawns.

Pour the rum mixture into the pan and allow to bubble for 30–40 seconds, stirring. Season with salt. Mix together the parsley and coriander. Pour the sauce over the prawns and scatter with the herbs before serving.

Serves 4

Tempura with soy and ginger dipping sauce

200 g (7 oz) shelled large prawns
  (shrimp), peeled and deveined,
  tails intact
300 g (10½ oz) skinned haddock
  fillets
2 teaspoons finely grated fresh ginger
1 tablespoon mirin
100 ml (3½ fl oz) soy sauce
vegetable oil, for deep-frying
250 g (2 cups) tempura flour (see
  Note)
1 large egg, lightly beaten
270 ml (1 cup and 1 tablespoon)
  iced water

Fish substitution
  bream, cod, rock cod, squid,
  lobster, crayfish

Make three cuts on the underside of each prawn and straighten them out. Cut the fish into bite-sized chunks.

Mix the ginger and mirin into the soy sauce, and dilute to taste with up to 2½ tablespoons of water. Pour the sauce into dipping bowls.

Fill a deep-fat fryer or large saucepan one-third full of oil and heat to 180°C (350°F), or until a cube of white bread dropped into the oil turns golden brown in 15 seconds.

Put the flour into a large bowl. Whisk the egg into the iced water. Very lightly whisk the iced water and egg into the tempura flour—it should still be lumpy. If you overwork the batter at this stage, you will not end up with a light coating. Dip the prawns and fish in the batter in batches and fry until crisp and golden. Drain on crumpled paper towels and serve immediately with the dipping sauce.

Serves 4

Note: Tempura flour is an especially fine flour available at Asian supermarkets. If you can't find it, use 185 g (1½ cups) plain (all-purpose) flour with 90 g (½ cup) rice flour.

Oyster po' boys

60 g (½ cup) self-raising flour
¼ teaspoon cayenne pepper
¼ teaspoon paprika
1 small egg
125 ml (½ cup) milk
vegetable oil, for deep-frying
18 oysters, shucked

Sift the flour, cayenne pepper, paprika and a pinch of salt into a bowl. Beat the egg and milk together and gradually add to the flour, whisking to give a smooth batter.

Fill a deep-fat fryer or large saucepan one-third full of oil and heat to 180°C (350°F), or until a cube of white bread dropped into the oil turns golden brown in 15 seconds. Pat dry the oysters, dip into the batter, and deep-fry in batches for 1–2 minutes, or until golden brown. Drain on crumpled paper towels and serve immediately either as they are or sandwiched between crusty bread.

Makes 18

Cajun 'popcorn'

1 egg
250 ml (1 cup) milk
90 g ($^3/_4$ cup) plain (all-purpose) flour
35 g ($^1/_4$ cup) fine cornmeal
$^1/_2$ teaspoon baking powder
1$^1/_2$ teaspoons Cajun spice mix
$^1/_4$ teaspoon dried basil
$^1/_2$ teaspoon celery salt
oil, for deep-frying
1 kg (2 lb 4 oz) prawns (shrimp),
    peeled and deveined
mayonnaise, for serving

Beat the egg and milk together. Sift the flour into a large bowl, then add the cornmeal, baking powder, Cajun spice mix, basil and celery salt. Make a well in the centre, gradually add half the beaten egg mixture and whisk until you have a smooth paste. Add the remaining egg mixture, mix well and leave to stand for 30 minutes to rest the batter and allow the starch to expand.

Fill a deep-fat fryer or large saucepan one-third full of oil and heat to 180°C (350°F), or until a cube of white bread dropped in the oil browns in 15 seconds.

Pat dry the prawns with paper towels. Dip the prawns in the batter and allow any excess batter to drain off. Cook in small batches in the oil until crisp and lightly golden. Remove with a slotted spoon or strainer and drain on crumpled paper towels. Serve hot with mayonnaise or another dipping sauce of your choice.

Serves 6

Gravlax

55 g (¼ cup) sugar
2 tablespoons coarse sea salt
1 teaspoon crushed black
  peppercorns
2.5 kg (5½ lb) good-quality salmon,
  filleted, skin on
1 tablespoon vodka or brandy
2 tablespoons very finely chopped dill
2 tablespoons chopped dill, extra

Mustard sauce
125 ml (½ cup) olive oil
2 tablespoons Dijon mustard
1½ tablespoons cider vinegar
2 teaspoons chopped dill
1 teaspoon caster (superfine) sugar

Combine the sugar, salt and
peppercorns in a small dish.

Remove any pinbones from the
salmon with tweezers or your fingers.
Pat dry with paper towels and lay a
fillet skin-side down in a shallow tray.
Sprinkle the fish with half the vodka,
rub half the sugar mixture into the
flesh, then sprinkle with 2 tablespoons
of the dill. Sprinkle the flesh side of
the other salmon fillet with the
remaining vodka and then rub the
remaining sugar mixture into the flesh.
Lay it flesh-side down on top of the
other fillet. Cover with plastic wrap,
place a heavy board on top and
weigh the board down with three
heavy tins so that the salmon is being
flattened. Refrigerate for 24 hours,
carefully turning it over after 12 hours.

For the mustard sauce, whisk all the
ingredients together.

Uncover the salmon and lay both
fillets on a board. Brush off all the
dill and seasoning using a stiff pastry
brush. Sprinkle with the extra dill and
press it onto the flesh, shaking off any
excess. Serve whole or thinly sliced
on an angle towards the tail, with the
mustard sauce.

Serves 12

Smoked salmon and rocket salad

Dressing
2 tablespoons extra virgin olive oil
1 tablespoon balsamic vinegar

150 g (1 bunch) rocket (arugula)
   leaves
1 avocado
250 g (9 oz) smoked salmon slices
325 g (11½ oz) marinated goat's
   cheese, drained and crumbled
2 tablespoons roasted hazelnuts,
   roughly chopped

Fish substitution
   smoked trout

For the dressing, thoroughly whisk together the oil and vinegar in a bowl. Season to taste.

Trim the long stems from the rocket. Rinse the leaves, pat dry and gently toss in a bowl with the dressing.

Cut the avocado into wedges. Put about three wedges on each serving plate with the salmon and rocket. Scatter the cheese and nuts over the top and season with freshly ground black pepper.

Serves 4

Taramasalata

5 slices of white bread, crusts
  removed
80 ml (1/3 cup) milk
100 g (31/2 oz) tarama (grey mullet roe)
1 egg yolk
1/2 small onion, grated
1 garlic clove, crushed
2 tablespoons lemon juice
80 ml (1/3 cup) olive oil
bread, for serving

Fish substitution
  smoked cod's roe

Soak the bread in the milk for
10 minutes. Press in a strainer to
extract any excess milk, then mix the
bread in a food processor with the
tarama, egg yolk, onion and garlic for
30 seconds, or until smooth. Mix in
1 tablespoon of the lemon juice.

With the motor running, slowly pour
in the olive oil until the mixture is
smooth. Add the remaining lemon
juice and a pinch of white pepper. If
the dip tastes too salty, add another
piece of bread and blend it together.
Serve the dip with bread.

Makes 11/2 cups

Blini with caviar

400 ml (14 fl oz) hand-hot milk
3 teaspoons dried yeast
175 g (1 cup and a heaped ⅓ cup)
   plain (all-purpose) flour
50 g (heaped ⅓ cup) buckwheat flour
2 large eggs, separated
70 g (2½ oz) butter
150 ml (5 fl oz) oil
275 g (9¾ oz) sour cream
200 g (7 oz) caviar

Fish substitution
   salmon roe, lumpfish roe

Pour half the milk into a jug, sprinkle on the yeast and a tablespoon of the plain flour and whisk well. Leave for 15 minutes until it froths.

Sift the flours and ¼ teaspoon salt into a large bowl. Add the yeast mixture and the remaining milk. Mix until you have a smooth batter. Cover with a damp tea towel and leave in a warm place until the mixture doubles in size and bubbles, which will take between 1 and 1½ hours.

Whisk the egg whites until stiff peaks form. Stir the egg yolks into the batter, then fold in the egg whites. Cover and leave again to rise for 10 minutes. Pour the mixture into a jug.

Heat one-third of the butter and 2 tablespoons of the oil in a large frying pan and add 1½ tablespoons batter. Cook for 30–60 seconds, or until small bubbles appear in the blini and it begins to turn golden. Flip it over and cook for 1–2 minutes on the other side. Repeat with the remaining batter, adding more butter and oil as needed. Top each blini with sour cream and a little caviar.

Serves 8

Scallop ceviche

16 scallops, in their shells, cleaned
1 teaspoon finely grated lime zest
60 ml (1/4 cup) lime juice
2 garlic cloves, chopped
2 red chillies, deseeded and chopped
1 tablespoon chopped coriander
   (cilantro) leaves
1 tablespoon olive oil
whole coriander (cilantro) leaves,
   for serving

Take the scallops off their shells, but don't throw away the shells.

In a non-metallic bowl, mix together the lime zest and juice, garlic, chilli, chopped coriander and the olive oil, and season with salt and pepper. Put the scallops in the dressing and stir to coat. Cover with plastic wrap and refrigerate for 2 hours. The acid from the lime juice will 'cold-cook' the scallop meat, turning it white.

To serve, slide each scallop back onto a half shell and spoon a little of the lime dressing over each of the scallops. Top each one with a coriander leaf. Serve cold.

Serves 4

Thai fish cakes

450 g (1 lb) skinned firm white fish
  fillets, such as cod or hake
45 g (¼ cup) rice flour
1 tablespoon fish sauce
1 egg, lightly beaten
3 tablespoons coriander (cilantro)
  leaves
3 teaspoons red curry paste
1–2 teaspoons chopped red chillies
  (optional)
100 g (3½ oz) green beans, very
  thinly sliced
2 spring onions (scallions), finely
  chopped
oil, for frying
sweet chilli sauce, for serving
chopped peanuts and finely diced
  cucumber (optional), for garnish

Fish substitution
  ling, redfish

Roughly chop the fish into chunks,
then process in a food processor for
20 seconds, or until smooth.

Add the rice flour, fish sauce,
egg, coriander leaves, curry paste
and chillies, if using. Process for
10 seconds, or until well combined,
then transfer to a large bowl.
Alternatively, finely chop and blend
by hand. Mix in the green beans and
spring onion. With wet hands, form
2 tablespoons of mixture at a time
into flattish patties.

Heat the oil in a heavy-based frying
pan over medium heat. Cook four fish
cakes at a time until golden brown on
both sides. Drain on crumpled paper
towels, then serve with sweet chilli
sauce. The sauce can be garnished
with a sprinkle of chopped peanuts
and finely diced cucumber.

Serves 4–6

Oysters with ginger and lime

12 oysters, shucked, in their shells
1/2 teaspoon finely grated fresh ginger
zest and juice of 2 limes
2 teaspoons Thai fish sauce
1 tablespoon chopped coriander
  (cilantro) leaves
2 teaspoons sugar
lime wedges, for serving

Nestle the opened oysters on a bed of crushed ice or rock salt on a large platter (this will keep them steady).

Mix the ginger, lime zest and juice, fish sauce, coriander and sugar together. Drizzle a little of the sauce into each oyster shell and serve with lime wedges.

Serves 2

Sardine patties

450 g (1 lb) sardines, gutted
1 thick slice of white bread, crusts
  removed
1 large garlic clove, crushed
2 tablespoons chopped parsley
pinch of ground cumin
pinch of ground paprika
2 large eggs, lightly beaten
40 g (⅓ cup) plain (all-purpose) flour,
  plus a little extra, for dusting
3–4 tablespoons oil
lemon wedges, for serving

Fish substitution
  herring, mackerel

Cut each sardine into two fillets and
remove the flesh from the skins.
Remove as many of the bones as
possible using tweezers. Roughly
chop the flesh and put in a bowl.

Put the bread in a food processor
and whiz to fine breadcrumbs or chop
finely by hand. Add the fish, garlic,
parsley, cumin, paprika, beaten egg
and flour and process until roughly
combined. Season with salt and mix.
With lightly floured hands, form the
mixture into six balls and place on a
plate. Cover and chill in the fridge for
30 minutes before cooking.

Heat the oil in a large frying pan and,
when hot, add three of the balls of
mixture. Once in the pan flatten them
out slightly to a patty shape. Cook
for 4–5 minutes on each side, or until
golden brown and cooked through.
Drain on crumpled paper towels and
keep warm. Repeat with the rest of
the balls, adding more oil if necessary.
Serve with the lemon wedges.

Makes 6

Steamed clams with corn and bacon

25 g (1 oz) butter
1 large onion, chopped
100 g (3½ oz) bacon, chopped
1.5 kg (3 lb 5 oz) fresh clams, cleaned
1 large cob of corn, kernels removed
150 ml (5 fl oz) dry cider
150 ml (5 fl oz) thick (double/heavy)
  cream

Fish substitution
  pipis, cockles, mussels

Melt the butter in a large saucepan and, when hot, add the onion and bacon. Cook over medium heat for about 5 minutes, or until the onion is soft and the bacon is cooked.

Tip the clams into a large saucepan with 60 ml (¼ cup) water and place over medium–high heat. Once the water is hot and the clams begin to steam, cover with a lid and cook for 2–3 minutes, or until they have opened. Drain, reserving the liquid, then strain the liquid through a fine sieve. Discard any clams that have not opened.

Add the corn kernels to the onion and bacon and cook for 3–4 minutes, or until tender, stirring. Pour in the cider and 60 ml (¼ cup) of the reserved clam cooking liquid. Bring to the boil, then simmer for 2 minutes. Stir in the cream, and season with salt and pepper. Tip in the clams and toss them in the sauce. Serve in warmed deep bowls.

Serves 4

King prawns with garlic, chilli and parsley

25 g (1 oz) butter
100 ml (3½ fl oz) olive oil
2 large garlic cloves, finely chopped
1 small red chilli, deseeded and finely
  chopped
16 king prawns (shrimp)
3 tablespoons chopped flat-leaf
  (Italian) parsley
lemon wedges, for serving

Fish substitution
  tiger prawns (shrimp)

Heat the butter and oil together in a large frying pan and, when hot, add the garlic and chilli. Cook, stirring all the time, for 30 seconds. Add the prawns and cook for 3–4 minutes on each side, or until they turn pink.

Sprinkle the prawns with the parsley and serve immediately on hot plates with the lemon wedges to squeeze over them.

Serves 4

Note: If you like you can heat up individual iron or stoneware dishes, transfer the just cooked prawns to them and serve the prawns still sizzling. Remember to provide finger bowls and napkins.

Crab cakes with avocado salsa

350 g (12 oz) fresh crab meat
2 eggs, lightly beaten
1 spring onion (scallion), finely
  chopped
1 tablespoon mayonnaise
2 teaspoons sweet chilli sauce
100 g (1¼ cups) fresh white
  breadcrumbs
oil, for shallow-frying
plain (all-purpose) flour, for dusting
lime wedges, for serving

Avocado salsa
2 ripe Roma (plum) tomatoes,
  chopped
1 small red onion, finely chopped
1 large ripe avocado, diced
60 ml (¼ cup) lime juice
2 tablespoons chervil leaves
½ teaspoon caster (superfine) sugar

Fish substitution
  tinned crab meat

Pick over the crab meat and pull out any stray pieces of shell or cartilage. Combine the crab meat, eggs, spring onion, mayonnaise, sweet chilli sauce and breadcrumbs in a bowl, season with salt and black pepper, then stir well. Using wet hands, form the crab mixture into eight small flat patties. Cover and put in the fridge for 30 minutes.

For the avocado salsa, put the tomato, onion, avocado, lime juice, chervil leaves and sugar in a bowl. Season to taste with salt and freshly ground black pepper, and toss gently to combine.

Heat the oil in a large frying pan over medium heat. Dust the crab cakes with flour and cook for 3 minutes on each side, or until golden brown— only turn them once so they don't break up. Drain on crumpled paper towels. Serve the crab cakes with the avocado salsa and lime wedges.

Serves 4

Sugar cane prawns with dipping sauce

Prawn mix
400 g (14 oz) prawns (shrimp),
 peeled and deveined
1 egg white
1 teaspoon ground coriander
2 red Asian shallots, peeled and
 roughly chopped
3 garlic cloves, peeled and
 roughly chopped
1 teaspoon grated palm sugar or
 soft brown sugar
1 teaspoon fish sauce
1 stem of lemon grass, white part
 only, cut into three pieces
1 tablespoon chopped Vietnamese
 mint or other mint leaves
1 teaspoon salt

Cucumber dipping sauce
1 tablespoon rice vinegar
1 tablespoon lime juice
1 tablespoon fish sauce
¼ teaspoon sambal oelek (see Notes)
1 teaspoon sugar
1 tablespoon finely chopped,
 peeled cucumber

15 x 10 cm (4 inch) lengths
 of thin sugar cane (approximately
 1 cm/½ inch diameter), peeled
 (see Notes)
oil, for deep-frying

Put the prawns in a food processor with half the egg white and all of the remaining ingredients for the prawn mix. Process to a paste. Alternatively, chop finely and mix by hand. Add just enough of the remaining egg white to bind the mixture. Tip the mixture out onto a large plate. Cover and chill for 30 minutes in the fridge.

Mix all the ingredients for the dipping sauce together in a small bowl.

Put a tablespoon of the prawn mixture in the palm of your hand. Press the end of a piece of sugar cane into the middle of the mixture, then firmly mould the mixture in your palm around the cane so that it covers about 6 cm (2$\frac{1}{2}$ inches) of the cane. Transfer to a board and repeat with the remaining prawn mixture and pieces of cane so that you have 15 sugar cane prawns in total.

Fill a deep-fat fryer or large saucepan one-third full of oil. Heat the oil to 180°C (350°F), or until a small cube of white bread dropped into the oil turns golden brown in 15 seconds.

Cook three prawn sticks at a time for 4–5 minutes, or until the prawn mixture turns a light golden brown. Turn halfway through cooking to ensure they brown evenly. Remove

from the oil using tongs and drain on paper towels. Cool for a few minutes before serving. Serve with the bowl of dipping sauce.

Makes 15

Notes: Sambal oelek is a hot paste made from fresh red chillies and other seasonings. It is sold in jars in the Asian section of the supermarket and it will keep for months if stored in the refrigerator.

It is nearly impossible to find fresh pieces of sugar cane. Packaged canes are sold in some speciality stores and have been boiled before being packaged to make them edible. Peel away the brownish skin from the white flesh before using.

Clams in yellow bean sauce

1 tablespoon oil
2 garlic cloves, crushed
1 tablespoon grated fresh ginger
2 tablespoons yellow bean sauce
    (see Note)
1.5 kg (3 lb 5 oz) hard-shelled clams,
    cleaned
125 ml (½ cup) chicken stock
1 spring onion (scallion), finely
    chopped

Fish substitution
    any type of clam

Heat a wok until very hot, add the oil and heat until hot. Stir-fry the garlic and ginger for 30 seconds, then add the yellow bean sauce and clams, and toss together. Add the chicken stock and stir until the clams have all opened, discarding any that do not open after 3 minutes. Season with salt and white pepper. Transfer the clams to a bowl or plate and sprinkle with the spring onion.

Serves 4

Note: Yellow bean sauce is sometimes called fermented yellow soy bean paste. It is sold in jars in the Asian section of the supermarket. If yellow bean sauce is unavailable, use the similarly flavoured brown bean sauce or the stronger flavoured black bean sauce.

Salmon carpaccio

500 g (1 lb 2 oz) sashimi-grade piece
  of salmon
3 vine-ripened tomatoes
1 tablespoon baby capers, rinsed
  and squeezed dry
1 tablespoon chopped dill
1 tablespoon extra virgin olive oil
1 tablespoon lime juice
crusty bread, for serving

Fish substitution
  fresh tuna, smoked salmon

Wrap the salmon piece in foil and freeze for 20–30 minutes, or until partly frozen.

Meanwhile, cut a cross in the base of each tomato, put in a bowl and cover with boiling water. Stand for 30 seconds, then plunge under cold water and peel the skin away from the cross. Cut each tomato in half, scoop out the seeds with a teaspoon and dice the flesh. Put the flesh in a bowl and stir in the capers and dill.

Remove the salmon from the freezer and unwrap. Using a very sharp knife or a mandolin, carefully cut the salmon into thin slices across the grain. Cover four serving plates with the slices in a thin layer. Alternatively, you can serve the salmon on a platter.

Whisk together the olive oil and lime juice in a small bowl and season with a large pinch of salt or sea salt. Drizzle this dressing over the salmon just before serving. Season with pepper and serve immediately with the tomato mixture and bread.

Serves 4

Tandoori-style prawns

3/4 teaspoon saffron threads
1 small onion, quartered
3 garlic cloves, peeled
2 teaspoons grated fresh ginger
2 tablespoons lemon juice
1/2 teaspoon chilli powder
1 teaspoon paprika
pinch of ground coriander
pinch of ground cumin
2 teaspoons garam masala
1–2 drops red food colouring for
    colour (optional)
1 tablespoon oil
200 g (7 oz) Greek-style yoghurt
30 prawns (shrimp), peeled and
    deveined, tails intact
lemon wedges and naan bread, for
    serving

Fish substitution
    chunks of sea bream, Murray cod,
    sea bass

Soak the saffron in 1 tablespoon hot water for 5 minutes. Add the saffron and its soaking liquid to a food processor with the onion, garlic, ginger, lemon juice, chilli powder, paprika, coriander, cumin, garam masala, food colouring (if using), oil and 1 teaspoon salt. Process to a paste. Scoop into a bowl and stir in the yoghurt.

Thread five prawns onto each of six metal skewers (if you're using bamboo skewers, soak them in water for 30 minutes first). Put in a non-metallic ovenproof dish (pick one that will fit in your oven) and cover with the marinade. Cover with plastic wrap and refrigerate for 2–3 hours. Allow the prawns to come to room temperature. Preheat the oven to 230°C (450°F/Gas 8). Remove the plastic wrap from the dish, then bake the prawns in the dish for 5–10 minutes, or until cooked.

Remove the skewers from the marinade (they will be very hot) and put on a foil-lined baking tray. Cook under a hot griller (broiler) for 2 minutes on each side, or until lightly browned and the marinade has dried up. Serve with lemon wedges and naan bread.

Serves 6

Seafood terrine

400 g (14 oz) skinned pike fillet,
  cut into bite-sized pieces and
  well chilled
2 large egg whites
225 ml (slightly less than 1 cup)
  thick (double/heavy) cream
1 tablespoon lemon juice
1 tablespoon chopped dill
1 teaspoon chopped chives
pinch of freshly grated nutmeg
115 g (4 oz) skinned salmon fillet
  cut into short, thin strips

Fish substitution
  cod or carp (instead of the pike),
  trout (instead of the salmon)

Line a loaf tin (22 x 7 x 7 cm/
$8^3/_4$ x $2^3/_4$ x $2^3/_4$ inches) with baking
paper and lightly oil the paper. Using
a food processor, blend the pike to a
smooth paste. Add the egg whites,
cream, lemon juice, dill and chives,
and process briefly using the pulse
button. Season with nutmeg, salt and
white pepper.

Preheat the oven to 180°C (350°F/
Gas 4). Transfer half of the pike
mixture to the loaf tin. Lay the salmon
strips on top, all facing the same
direction crossways so the terrine will
cut easily. Season with salt and white
pepper and cover with the remaining
pike mixture. Cover with foil and place
in a roasting tin. Add boiling water to
the roasting tin until one-third of the
loaf tin is immersed in water.

Bake for 40–45 minutes, or until firm
to the touch. Remove the tin from the
water and leave until cold. Chill
overnight in the fridge. Lay a large
plate over the top of the tin and invert
it so that the terrine comes out onto
the plate. Peel off the paper and serve
in slices. Great with a watercress and
cucumber salad.

Serves 6

Moules marinières

50 g (1¾ oz) butter
1 large onion, chopped
½ celery stalk, chopped
2 garlic cloves, crushed
400 ml (14 fl oz) white wine
1 bay leaf
2 thyme sprigs
2 kg (4½ lb) mussels, cleaned
220 ml (slightly less than 1 cup) thick
  (double/heavy) cream
2 tablespoons chopped parsley
bread, for serving

Melt the butter in a large saucepan over medium heat. Add the onion, celery and garlic and cook, stirring occasionally, for about 5 minutes, or until the onion is softened but not browned.

Add the wine, bay leaf and thyme to the saucepan and bring to the boil. Add the mussels, cover the pan tightly and simmer over low heat for 2–3 minutes, shaking the pan occasionally. Use tongs to lift out the mussels as they open and put them into a warm dish. Throw away any mussels that haven't opened after 3 minutes.

Strain the liquid through a fine sieve lined with muslin into a clean saucepan, to get rid of any grit or sand. Bring to the boil and boil for 2 minutes. Add the cream and reheat the sauce without boiling. Season well. Serve the mussels in individual bowls with the liquid poured over. Sprinkle with the parsley and serve with plenty of bread.

Serves 6

Spicy fish cakes

2 small dried red chillies, stalks
  removed
14 pieces of banana leaf measuring
  16 x 12 cm (6½ x 5 inches)
  (see Note)
450 g (1 lb) groper fillets, skinned and
  cut into chunks
1 stem of lemon grass, cut into three
  pieces
1 small onion, cut in half
1 large garlic clove, peeled
generous pinch of ground turmeric
1 teaspoon grated palm sugar or soft
  brown sugar
1 teaspoon ground coriander
1 teaspoon shrimp paste
1 tablespoon candlenuts or unsalted
  macadamias or peanuts
1 tablespoon chopped mint
1 tablespoon chopped coriander
  (cilantro) leaves
60 ml (¼ cup) coconut milk

Fish substitution
  hapuka, blue warehou, halibut,
  haddock, snapper

Soak the chillies in boiling water. Soak
14 cocktail sticks in cold water. If you
are using fresh banana leaves, blanch
them in boiling water for a minute,
then drain and refresh in cold water.

Put the fish in a food processor and
blend to a thick purée. Scoop into a
bowl. Drain the chillies and put in
the processor along with the rest of
the ingredients and a pinch of salt.
Blend to a paste. Add the paste to
the fish and mix well.

Drain the cocktail sticks. Put about
2 tablespoons of mixture in the middle
of each piece of banana leaf. Fold the
shorter sides of the rectangle into
the middle so they overlap. Tuck the
two protruding ends underneath to
make a small package. Secure the
two ends with a cocktail stick. Put
the parcels smooth-side down on
a barbecue hotplate or heated frying
pan and cook for 5 minutes, or until
the banana leaf has lightly browned
and the parcels are hot in the middle.
Unwrap before eating.

Makes 14

Note: You can buy banana leaves
from Asian food stores and speciality
fruit and vegetable shops. Foil can be
used instead.

Drunken prawns

24 large prawns (shrimp), peeled
and deveined
150 ml (5 fl oz) Chinese rice wine
(see Note)
2 red chillies, thinly sliced
1 teaspoon finely grated fresh ginger
2 teaspoons sugar

Put the prawns in a non-metallic
bowl. Mix the rice wine with the
chillies, ginger and sugar and pour
over the prawns. Leave to marinate
for 30 minutes.

Heat a wok until very hot. Take
60 ml (1/4 cup) of the rice wine out
of the marinade and add to the wok.
Heat it until it is very hot, then light
it either with a match or by tipping
the side of the wok towards the gas
flame. Let the flame burn and die
down before adding the rest of the
marinade and prawns. Cook for
2–3 minutes, or until the prawns
turn pink. Serve immediately.

Serves 4

Note: Chinese rice wine is a
fermented rice wine with a rich,
sweetish taste, similar to dry sherry.
It is sometimes called Shaoxing
rice wine.

Stir-fried crabs with tamarind sauce

2 large or 4 small live mud crabs
60 ml (¼ cup) oil
2 large garlic cloves, crushed
2 small red chillies, deseeded and
  finely chopped

Tamarind sauce
60 ml (¼ cup) sweet chilli sauce
1 tablespoon Thai fish sauce
2 tablespoons soy sauce
2 tablespoons tamarind purée or
  lemon juice
25 g (1 oz) grated palm sugar or soft
  brown sugar
250 ml (1 cup) coconut milk
1 tablespoon water

Fish substitution
  other types of crab such as
  blue swimmer

Freeze the crabs for 1 hour to immobilize them. Plunge them into boiling water for 2 minutes, then drain. Wash well with a stiff brush, then pat dry. Pull the apron back from underneath the crab and separate the shells. Remove the feathery gills and intestines. Twist off the claws. Using a cleaver or large knife, cut the crabs in half. Crack the claws using crab crackers or the back of a heavy knife.

Heat 2 tablespoons of the oil in a wok until just beginning to smoke. Carefully add half of the crab pieces. Stir for 1 minute, reduce the heat to medium and cover with a lid. Cook for 5–7 minutes, or until the crab shells turn bright red. Lift onto a plate, then repeat with the rest of the crab.

Mix together the ingredients for the tamarind sauce in a jug. Add the last of the oil to the wok and, when hot, add the garlic and chillies. Cook for a minute, stirring, then add the sauce mixture. Bring to the boil, then reduce the heat to medium and leave to bubble away, without a lid, for 8–10 minutes, or until you have a thick sauce. Return the crab to the wok and stir to coat in the sauce. Remove to a serving plate and spoon the sauce over the top.

Serves 4

Salt-and-pepper squid

1 kg (2 lb 4 oz) squid tubes, halved
  lengthways
250 ml (1 cup) lemon juice
250 g (2 cups) cornflour (cornstarch)
1 1/2 tablespoons salt
1 tablespoon ground white pepper
2 teaspoons caster (superfine) sugar
4 egg whites, lightly beaten
oil, for deep-frying
lemon wedges, for serving
coriander (cilantro) leaves, for garnish

Open out the squid tubes, wash and
pat dry. Lay on a chopping board with
the inside facing upwards. Score a
fine diamond pattern on the squid,
being careful not to cut all the way
through. Cut into pieces about
5 x 3 cm (2 x 1 1/4 inches). Place
in a flat non-metallic dish and pour
the lemon juice over the top. Cover
and refrigerate for 15 minutes. Drain
and pat dry.

Combine the cornflour, salt, white
pepper and sugar in a bowl. Dip the
squid into the egg white and then
into the flour mixture, shaking off
any excess.

Fill a deep-fat fryer or large saucepan
one-third full of oil and heat to 180°C
(350°F), or until a small cube of white
bread dropped into the oil turns
golden brown in 15 seconds. Cook
batches of the squid for 1–2 minutes,
or until the flesh turns white and curls.
Drain on crumpled paper towels.
Serve with lemon wedges and garnish
with coriander.

Serves 6

Smoked trout pâté

2 whole smoked trout
200 g (7 oz) cream cheese
2 tablespoons finely chopped dill
juice of ½ lemon
pinch of cayenne pepper
toast, for serving
lemon wedges, for serving

Fish substitution
   4 smoked trout fillets, skinned

Skin the smoked trout, remove the heads and skin, then lift the flesh off the bones. Break the flesh into flakes and put in a bowl or food processor. Either mash the flesh with a fork or briefly process until it is broken up, but still with plenty of texture.

Beat the cream cheese with a wooden spoon until soft. Add the smoked trout flesh and mix everything together well. Stir in the dill and lemon juice, then season with salt, pepper and cayenne pepper.

Chill the pâté until you need it but bring it to room temperature before serving or the cream cheese may cause it to go too solid. Serve with Melba or brown toast. Provide extra lemon wedges to squeeze over.

Serves 6

Oysters with vinegar and shallots

24 oysters, shucked, in their shells
1 French shallot, finely chopped
2 tablespoons red wine vinegar
rye bread and butter, for serving
(optional)

Nestle the opened oysters on a bed of crushed ice or rock salt on a large platter (this will keep them steady).

Mix the chopped shallot with the red wine vinegar and some freshly ground black pepper in a small bowl. Put this in the centre of the platter. The oysters are eaten with a little of the vinegar and shallots poured over them. Serve with buttered rye bread, if desired.

Serves 4

Garlic prawns

1.25 kg (2 lb 12 oz) prawns (shrimp),
  peeled and deveined, tails intact
85 g (3 oz) butter, melted
185 ml (¾ cup) olive oil
8 garlic cloves, crushed
2 spring onions (scallions), thinly
  sliced
crusty bread, for serving

Preheat the oven to 250°C (500°F/ Gas 9). Cut a slit down the back of each prawn.

Combine the butter and oil and divide among four 500 ml (2 cup) cast-iron pots. Divide half the crushed garlic among the pots.

Place the pots on a baking tray and heat in the oven for 4 minutes, or until the mixture is bubbling. Remove and divide the prawns and remaining garlic among the pots. Return to the oven for 5 minutes, or until the prawns are cooked. Stir in the spring onion. Season to taste. Serve with crusty bread to mop up the juices.

Serves 4

Steamed prawn banana leaf cups

16 x 10 cm (4 inch) circles of banana
   leaf or 8 cups each with a 100 ml
   (3½ fl oz) capacity
300 g (10½ oz) prawns (shrimp),
   peeled and deveined
1 small red chilli, deseeded
2 teaspoons red curry paste
3 cm (1¼ inch) piece of lemon grass,
   roughly chopped
1 large egg
60 ml (¼ cup) coconut cream
1 tablespoon fish sauce
¼ teaspoon sugar
2 tablespoons unsalted peanuts

Begin by making eight banana leaf
cups. Place two banana leaf circles
together to make a double layer.
Make four small tucks around the
circle, stapling them to secure as
you go, to create a banana leaf 'cup'.
Repeat for the other seven cups.
Alternatively you can use eight 100 ml
(3½ fl oz) ramekins. Either way, also
cut out eight 7 cm (2¾ inch) circles of
baking paper.

Tip the prawns into a food processor
with the chilli, curry paste, lemon
grass, egg, coconut cream, fish
sauce, sugar and half of the peanuts.
Blend to a rough paste.

Evenly divide the mixture among the
cups. Place a circle of baking paper
on the top of each one. Place in a
bamboo or metal steamer, cover and
steam for 10–12 minutes, or until the
mixture has risen and feels firm to the
touch. You may need to cook in two
batches. Remove the baking paper.

Meanwhile, lightly toast the remaining
peanuts. Cool a little, then roughly
chop. Serve each cup with a little of
the toasted peanuts scattered over
the top.

Makes 8

Everyday

Marinated and seared tuna

80 ml (1/3 cup) soy sauce
60 ml (1/4 cup) mirin
1 tablespoon sake
1 teaspoon caster (superfine) sugar
1 teaspoon finely grated fresh ginger
2 teaspoons lemon juice
4 x 175 g (6 oz) tuna steaks
1 tablespoon oil
coriander leaves, for garnish

Fish substitution
salmon

Mix the soy sauce, mirin, sake, sugar, ginger and lemon juice together in a jug. Put the tuna steaks in a shallow dish and spoon the marinade over the top. Turn the fish in the marinade, ensuring it is well coated. Cover and leave to marinate for 30 minutes in the fridge.

Preheat a chargrill pan or barbecue hotplate until hot. Lift the tuna out of the marinade and pour the marinade into a small saucepan. Bring the marinade to the boil and reduce for 1 minute.

Meanwhile, lightly oil the surface of the chargrill pan and add the tuna steaks. Cook for 2–3 minutes on each side so that the tuna is cooked on the outside but still pink in the middle. Serve with some of the marinade spooned over the top and garnished with coriander. Great with rice and steamed vegetables.

Serves 4

Tandoori prawn pizza

1 tablespoon olive oil
2 teaspoons ground paprika
1/2 teaspoon ground cumin
1/4 teaspoon ground cardamom
1/4 teaspoon ground ginger
1/4 teaspoon cayenne pepper
90 g (1/3 cup) Greek-style yoghurt,
  plus extra, for serving
1 teaspoon lemon juice
2 garlic cloves, crushed
16 prawns (shrimp), peeled
  and deveined, tails intact
30 cm (12 inch) ready-made pizza
  base
1 onion, sliced
1 small red capsicum (pepper), sliced
3 tablespoons torn basil

Preheat the oven to 220°C (425°F/ Gas 7). To make the tandoori sauce, heat the oil in a frying pan over medium heat, add the spices and cook until the oil starts to bubble, then cook for another minute. Stir in the yoghurt, lemon juice and garlic, then add the prawns. Cook for 5 minutes, or until the prawns are pink and cooked.

Remove the prawns from the tandoori sauce with a slotted spoon and spread the sauce over the pizza base, leaving a 1 cm (1/2 inch) border. Sprinkle with some of the onion and capsicum, then arrange all the prawns on top. Top with the remaining onion and capsicum and bake for about 20 minutes. Scatter with basil, then serve with the extra yoghurt.

Serves 4

John Dory with tarator sauce

Tarator sauce
140 g (1 cup) hazelnuts
2 slices of white bread, crusts
  removed
2 garlic cloves, roughly crushed
150 ml (5 fl oz) olive oil, plus a little
  extra for cooking
60 ml (1/4 cup) lemon juice

800 g (1 lb 12 oz) skinless John
  Dory fillets
lemon wedges, for serving

Fish substitution
  groper, snapper, halibut, cod,
  sea bass

To make the tarator sauce, put the hazelnuts in a food processor and grind finely. Briefly soak the bread in a small bowl of water. Squeeze dry, tear into pieces and add to the food processor bowl along with the garlic. Process briefly to combine. Mix the oil and lemon juice together in a jug and, with the processor motor running, gradually pour it into the bread and nut mixture. Season to taste with salt and pepper, then scoop the sauce into a serving bowl.

Heat a frying pan or chargrill pan until hot. Brush with a little oil and cook the fillets for 3 minutes on each side, or until the flesh is opaque and flakes easily. You may need to cook the fish in two batches; if so, keep the first batch warm, covered with foil, in a low oven. Serve the fish fillets with the tarator sauce and lemon wedges.

Serves 6

Note: Tarator sauce has its origins in Turkey. It is creamy and garlicky and can be made with walnuts, almonds or pine nuts instead of hazelnuts.

Blackened snapper

6 large skinless snapper fillets, 2 cm
  (³/₄ inch) thick
125 g (4½ oz) unsalted butter,
  melted
2 tablespoons Cajun spice mix
2 teaspoons sweet paprika
lemon wedges, for serving

Fish substitution
  blue-eye, ling, warehou, mahi mahi

Brush each fish fillet liberally with the
melted butter.

Combine the Cajun spice mix and
paprika, then sprinkle thickly over the
fish. Use your fingers to rub the spice
mix evenly over the fillets.

Heat a large frying pan over high heat.
Cook two fillets at a time in the pan
for 1–2 minutes on one side. Turn and
cook for another few minutes, or until
the fish is cooked and flakes easily.
The surface should be well charred
on each side. Add extra butter if
necessary. Serve drizzled with any
remaining melted butter and lemon
wedges—they can be served lightly
charred if you like.

Serves 6

Swordfish with bananas

2 tablespoons oil
1 onion, thinly sliced
1 small green capsicum (pepper),
   sliced
pinch of dried chilli flakes
pinch of freshly grated nutmeg
2 tomatoes
2 bananas
4 x 200 g (7 oz) swordfish steaks
250 ml (1 cup) coconut milk
coriander leaves, for garnish

Fish substitution
   tuna, halibut

Heat the oil in a large deep frying or sauté pan, then add the onion. Cook for 5 minutes, then add the green capsicum, chilli and nutmeg and cook for a further 3–4 minutes, or until the onion and pepper are soft.

Meanwhile, score a cross in the base of each tomato. Cover with boiling water for 30 seconds, then plunge into cold water. Drain and peel the skin away from the cross. Cut each one into quarters. Peel the bananas and cut into chunks on the diagonal.

Put the swordfish steaks in the pan on top of the onions and capsicum and scatter the tomato quarters and banana over the top. Pour the coconut milk into the pan and season with salt and pepper. Cover and cook gently for 15 minutes, or until the fish is cooked through (it should feel firm when it is ready). Garnish with coriander leaves and serve with rice.

Serves 4

Idaho trout parcels

25 g (1 oz) butter
1 tablespoon olive oil, plus a little for
the parcels
1 French shallot, finely chopped
225 g (8 oz) small mushrooms, sliced
2 tablespoons tarragon vinegar
1 tablespoon chopped tarragon
4 x 175–225 g (6–8 oz) pieces of
skinless trout

Fish substitution

John Dory, snapper, orange roughy

Preheat the oven to 220°C (425°F/ Gas 7). Heat the butter and oil in a frying pan, then cook the shallot for 2–3 minutes, or until softened. Add the mushrooms, then stir to coat them in the oil and butter and cook for 5 minutes, stirring every now and then. Splash in the vinegar and bubble away for 30 seconds. Take the pan off the heat and stir in the tarragon. Season with salt and freshly ground black pepper.

Lightly oil four 35 cm (14 inch) rounds of heavy-duty baking paper. Fold in half to make a crease in the middle and then unfold again. Lay them oil-side up. Put a piece of fish on one half of each circle. Top with the mushroom mixture, dividing it equally among the circles. Fold the empty half of the circle over the fish and fold the edges of the circle twice and pinch together to seal firmly. Do the same for each one. Lay the parcels on a large baking tray and bake for 10–15 minutes. Transfer the parcels to serving plates and let everyone open their own.

Serves 4

Fish Provençale

1 small red capsicum (pepper),
   thinly sliced
250 g (1 cup) bottled pasta sauce
1 tablespoon chopped thyme
40 g (1 1/2 oz) butter
4 large skinless perch fillets
thyme sprigs, for garnish

Fish substitution
   snapper

Put the capsicum, pasta sauce
and chopped thyme in a bowl and
mix well.

Melt half the butter in a large non-
stick frying pan over high heat and
cook the fish for 1 minute, adding the
remaining butter as you go. Turn the
fish over and pour on the capsicum
mixture. Simmer for 10 minutes, or
until the fish is cooked. Season to
taste and garnish with thyme sprigs.
Serve with roasted potato slices and
crusty bread to soak up the juices.

Serves 4

Baked swordfish steaks with salsa verde

4 x 200 g (7 oz) swordfish steaks

Salsa verde
2 tablespoons olive oil
1 large onion, finely chopped
1 garlic clove, finely chopped
1 large green capsicum (pepper)
40 g (1 ½ oz) jalapeño chillies
2 tablespoons roughly chopped
   coriander (cilantro) leaves

Fish substitution
   tuna, marlin, kingfish, barramundi

Preheat the oven to 180°C (350°F/ Gas 4). Put the swordfish steaks in a large rectangular ovenproof dish.

To make the salsa verde, heat 1 tablespoon of the oil in a small saucepan and, when hot, add the onion and garlic and cook for 10 minutes, or until the onion has softened. Allow to cool for a few minutes. Blanch the capsicum in boiling water for 8 minutes, then drain. Put the softened onion and garlic in a food processor with the capsicum, chillies, coriander and remaining oil. Blend to a purée and season with salt. Alternatively, finely chop the ingredients by hand and mix together well.

Spread the salsa verde on top of the swordfish steaks, dividing it equally. Bake in the preheated oven for 20–25 minutes, or until the fish is firm and opaque. Serve with crispy baked potato chunks.

Serves 4

Fish pie

Potato topping
500 g (1 lb 2 oz) floury potatoes
  (e.g. Idaho, King Edward), diced
60 ml (1/4 cup) milk or cream
1 egg, lightly beaten
30 g (1 oz) butter
60 g (2 1/4 oz) Cheddar cheese,
  finely grated

800 g (1 lb 12 oz) skinless ling fillets,
  cut into large chunks
375 ml (1 1/2 cups) milk
30 g (1 oz) butter
1 onion, finely chopped
1 garlic clove, crushed
2 tablespoons plain (all-purpose) flour
2 tablespoons lemon juice
2 teaspoons lemon zest
1 tablespoon chopped dill

Fish substitution
  snapper, monkfish, cod, haddock,
  flathead

Preheat the oven to 180°C (350°F/ Gas 4). To make the topping, steam the potatoes until tender. Mash, then push to one side of the pan, add the milk and heat gently. Beat the milk into the potato until it is fluffy, then season and stir in the egg and butter. Mix in half the Cheddar, then set aside and keep warm.

Put the fish in a frying pan and cover with the milk. Bring to the boil, then reduce the heat and simmer for 2 minutes, or until the fish is opaque and flaky. Drain, reserving the milk, and put the fish in a 1.5 litre (6 cup) ovenproof dish.

Melt the butter in a saucepan and cook the onion and garlic for 2 minutes. Stir in the flour and cook for 1 minute, or until pale and foaming. Remove from the heat and gradually stir in the reserved milk. Return to the heat and stir constantly until it boils and thickens. Reduce the heat and simmer for 2 minutes. Add the lemon juice, zest and dill, and season. Mix with the fish. Spoon the topping over the fish and top with the remaining Cheddar. Bake for 35 minutes, or until golden.

Serves 4

Jansson's temptation

15 anchovy fillets
80 ml (⅓ cup) milk
60 g (2¼ oz) butter
2 large onions, thinly sliced
5 potatoes, peeled, cut into
    5 mm (¼ mm) slices, then julienned
    (cut into matchsticks)
500 g (2 cups) thick
    (double/heavy) cream

Preheat the oven to 200°C (400°F/
Gas 6). Soak the anchovies in the milk
for 5 minutes to lessen their saltiness.
Drain and rinse.

Melt half the butter in a frying pan and
cook the onion over medium heat for
5 minutes, or until golden and tender.
Chop the remaining butter into small
cubes and set aside.

Spread half the potato over the base
of a shallow ovenproof dish, top with
the anchovies and onion and finish
with the remaining potato.

Pour half the cream over the potato
and scatter the butter cubes on top.
Bake for 20 minutes, or until golden.
Pour the remaining cream over the
top and cook for another 40 minutes,
or until the potato feels tender when
the point of a knife is inserted. Season
with salt and pepper before serving.

Serves 4

Stir-fried swordfish with bok choy

500 g (1 lb 2 oz) swordfish steaks,
  cut into bite-sized pieces
2 tablespoons freshly cracked black
  pepper
2 tablespoons hoisin sauce
2 tablespoons rice wine
1 tablespoon oyster sauce
1 tablespoon soy sauce
oil, for cooking
3 garlic cloves, thinly sliced
1 onion, sliced
1 kg (2 lb 4 oz) baby bok choy
  (pak choi), leaves separated
100 g (3½ oz) fresh shiitake
  mushrooms, sliced
1 tablespoon sesame seeds, toasted
1 teaspoon sesame oil

Fish substitution
  tuna

Coat the swordfish in cracked black pepper, then shake off any excess.

Combine the hoisin sauce, rice wine, oyster sauce and soy sauce in a small bowl or jug.

Heat a wok over high heat, add 2 tablespoons of the oil and swirl it around to coat the side of the wok. Stir-fry the swordfish in batches for 1–2 minutes each batch, or until tender. Be careful not to overcook the fish or it will break up. Remove from the wok.

Reheat the wok, add 1 tablespoon of the oil, then stir-fry the garlic for 30 seconds, or until crisp and golden. Add the onion and stir-fry for 1–2 minutes, or until golden. Add the bok choy and mushrooms and cook briefly until the leaves wilt. Pour the sauce into the wok and stir until everything is coated in the sauce.

Return the swordfish to the wok and toss everything together. Serve sprinkled with sesame seeds and drizzled with the sesame oil.

Serves 4

Mexican baked fish

3 tomatoes, chopped
½ teaspoon ground cumin
½ teaspoon ground allspice
½ teaspoon ground cinnamon
1 habanero chilli, deseeded and
  finely chopped
4 tablespoons coriander (cilantro)
  leaves
4 x 175–200 g (6–7 oz) skinless red
  snapper fillets
½ small red onion, chopped
½ small green capsicum (pepper),
  chopped
1 tablespoon sour or Seville orange
  juice, or 2 teaspoons orange juice
  and 2 teaspoons vinegar
juice of 1 lime

Fish substitution
  flake, grouper, cod

Preheat the oven to 190°C (375°F/ Gas 5). Mix the tomatoes in a bowl with the cumin, allspice, cinnamon, chilli and coriander.

Cut four squares of foil, each large enough to enclose a fish fillet. Put a piece of fish on each of the foil squares and divide the tomato mixture among the four fillets.

Mix the red onion and green capsicum together and divide among the parcels. Stir the orange and lime juice together and drizzle over the top of the fish and vegetables. Season with salt and pepper.

Wrap the fish in the foil and transfer the parcels to a baking dish. Bake for 15–20 minutes, or until the fish flakes easily when tested with a fork.

Serves 4

Baked bream with fennel

4 small fennel bulbs
40 g (1 1/2 oz) butter
2 tablespoons olive oil
2 onions, chopped
1 garlic clove, crushed
4 x 300 g (10 1/2 oz) whole bream,
  scaled and gutted
extra virgin olive oil
1 lemon, quartered
1 tablespoon oregano leaves
lemon wedges, for serving

Fish substitution

1 whole sea bass (cook for an
extra 10 minutes)

Preheat the oven to 190°C (375°F/ Gas 5) and grease a large shallow ovenproof dish. Thinly slice the fennel, reserving the green fronds.

Heat the butter and olive oil in a large frying pan and gently cook the fennel, onion and garlic for 12–15 minutes, or until softened but not browned. Season with salt and freshly ground black pepper.

Stuff each fish with a heaped tablespoon of the fennel mixture and a quarter of the fennel fronds. Brush with extra virgin olive oil, squeeze lemon over the top and season well.

Spoon the remainder of the cooked fennel into the ovenproof dish and sprinkle with half of the oregano. Lay the fish on top of the fennel. Sprinkle the remaining oregano over the fish and cover the dish loosely with foil. Bake for 15 minutes, or until just cooked through. Serve with a wedge of lemon.

Serves 4

Pan-fried rainbow trout with almonds

2 rainbow trout, scaled and gutted
plain (all-purpose) flour, for coating
60 g (2¼ oz) butter
1 tablespoon oil
25 g (¼ cup) flaked almonds
2 tablespoons lemon juice
1 tablespoon finely chopped parsley,
   plus some extra leaves, for garnish
lemon wedges, for serving

Fish substitution
   any type of trout

Wash the fish and pat dry with paper towels. Coat the fish with flour and season well on each side as well as inside. Heat half the butter and all of the oil in a large frying pan until it is very hot, then add the fish. Cook for 4 minutes on each side, or until golden brown and cooked through. Lift up one side of the fish to check if the flesh on the inside is opaque and cooked through. If cooked, the dorsal fin should pull out easily. Remove the fish and place on heated serving plates. Cover very loosely with foil and place in a warm oven.

Heat the remaining butter in a frying pan, add the flaked almonds and stir until the almonds turn light golden. Add the lemon juice and parsley, and season with salt and pepper. Stir until the sauce is heated through. Pour over the fish, garnish with parsley, then serve with lemon wedges.

Serves 2

Basic pan-fried fish

2–3 tablespoons plain
  (all-purpose) flour
4 blue-eye fish cutlets
olive oil, for shallow-frying

Fish substitution
  jewfish, warehou, snapper or other
  firm white fish

Sift the flour together with a little salt and freshly ground black pepper onto a plate. Pat the fish dry with paper towels, then coat both sides of the cutlets with seasoned flour, shaking off any excess.

Heat about 3 mm ($\frac{1}{8}$ inch) oil in a large frying pan until very hot. Put the fish into the hot oil and cook for 3 minutes on one side, then turn and cook the other side for 2 minutes, or until the coating is crisp and well browned. Reduce the heat to low and cook for another 2–3 minutes, or until the flesh flakes easily when tested with a fork.

Remove the fish from the pan and drain briefly on crumpled paper towels. If you are cooking in batches, keep warm while cooking the remaining cutlets. Serve immediately with a salad or steamed vegetables.

Serves 4

Fresh tuna and green bean stir-fry

300 g (10½ oz) small green beans, trimmed
2 tablespoons oil
600 g (1 lb 5 oz) piece of tuna, cut into small cubes
250 g (9 oz) punnet small cherry tomatoes
16 small black olives
2–3 tablespoons lemon juice
2 garlic cloves, finely chopped
8 anchovy fillets, rinsed, dried and finely chopped
3 tablespoons small basil leaves

Blanch the beans in a small saucepan of boiling water for 2 minutes. Drain and refresh under cold water, then set aside.

Heat a wok until very hot, add the oil and swirl it around to coat the side. Stir-fry the tuna in batches for about 5 minutes each batch, or until cooked on the outside but still a little pink on the inside.

Add the cherry tomatoes, olives and beans to the wok, then gently toss until heated through. Add the lemon juice, garlic and anchovies and stir well. Season to taste with salt and freshly ground black pepper. Serve scattered with the basil leaves.

Serves 4

Roast fish with rosemary and garlic

1 kg (2 lb 4 oz) skinless monkfish tail
    fillets, membrane removed, or
    barramundi fillets
3 large garlic cloves, peeled and
    sliced into thin slivers
1 stem of rosemary, cut into
    24 small sprigs
6 streaky bacon rashers, cut in half
80 ml (1/3 cup) olive oil
lemon wedges, for serving

Fish substitution
    cod, halibut, swordfish

Preheat the oven to 200°C (400°F/
Gas 6). Using a small sharp knife,
make small incisions in the fish and
insert a sliver of garlic and a small
sprig of rosemary into each one.
Season the fish with salt and pepper
and wrap a piece of bacon around
each piece of fish.

Put the fish in a roasting tin and
drizzle the olive oil over the top.
Roast for about 15 minutes, or until
the fish is cooked through. Serve
with lemon wedges.

Serves 4

African fish pie

25 g (1 oz) butter, plus a little extra,
   for greasing the tin
2 onions, finely chopped
2 garlic cloves, crushed
2 tablespoons mild curry powder
$\frac{1}{2}$ teaspoon turmeric
grated zest and juice of 1 small lemon
100 g ($3\frac{1}{2}$ oz) raisins
50 g ($\frac{1}{3}$ cup) whole blanched
   almonds, chopped
250 ml (1 cup) milk
40 g (approximately 2 thick slices)
   white bread
1 kg (2 lb 4 oz) skinless snook fillet,
   finely chopped
2 large eggs

Fish substitution
   pike, cod

Preheat the oven to 190°C (375°F/
Gas 5). Heat the butter in a frying
pan and add the onion. Cook for
7–8 minutes, or until soft and lightly
golden, stirring occasionally. Add
the garlic and cook for a further
2 minutes. Mix in 1 tablespoon of the
curry powder, the turmeric, lemon
zest and juice, raisins and almonds.
Remove from the heat and allow to
cool for 10 minutes.

Pour $2\frac{1}{2}$ tablespoons of the milk into
a bowl and soak the bread in it for
10 minutes, turning after 5 minutes.
Squeeze the bread dry, then tear into
small pieces and put in a bowl. Add
the fish, one of the eggs and the
mixture from the frying pan to the
bowl, season well and mix together.
Scoop into a lightly buttered non-stick
23 cm (9 inch) square tin that is
7 cm ($2\frac{3}{4}$ inches) high. Bake for
15 minutes. Towards the end of the
15 minutes, whisk together the
remaining milk, curry powder and
egg. Pour the liquid over the top of
the mixture in the tin. Bake for a
further 45 minutes, or until set. Cool
for 15 minutes, then cut into squares
to serve.

Serves 6

Steamed fish cutlets with ginger and chilli

4 x 175 g (6 oz) firm jewfish cutlets
5 cm (2 inch) piece of fresh ginger,
  shredded
2 garlic cloves, chopped
2 teaspoons chopped red chillies
2 tablespoons chopped coriander
  (cilantro) stalks
3 spring onions (scallions), cut into
  fine short shreds
2 tablespoons lime juice

Fish substitution
  snapper, blue-eye, cod

Line a bamboo steamer basket with banana leaves or baking paper to prevent the fish sticking to the base.

Arrange the fish in the steamer and top with the ginger, garlic, chilli and coriander stalks. Cover and steam over a wok or pan of boiling water for 8–10 minutes, or until the fish flakes easily. Sprinkle the spring onion and lime juice over the fish, cover and steam for an extra 30 seconds. Serve with steamed jasmine rice.

Serves 4

Baked tuna Siciliana

80 ml (⅓ cup) olive oil
2 tablespoons lemon juice
2½ tablespoons finely chopped basil
4 x 175 g (6 oz) tuna steaks
60 g (2¼ oz) black olives, pitted
  and chopped
1 tablespoon baby capers, rinsed and
  patted dry
2 anchovies, finely chopped
400 g (14 oz) tomatoes, peeled,
  deseeded and chopped, or a
  400 g (14 oz) tin chopped tomatoes
2 tablespoons dry breadcrumbs
bread, for serving

Fish substitution
  swordfish

Mix 2 tablespoons of the olive oil with the lemon juice and 1 tablespoon of the basil. Season and pour into a shallow, non-metallic ovenproof dish, large enough to hold the tuna steaks in a single layer. Arrange the tuna in the dish and leave to marinate for 15 minutes, turning once. Preheat the oven to 220°C (425°F/Gas 7) and preheat the griller (broiler).

Combine the olives, capers, anchovies and tomatoes with the remaining oil and the remaining basil and season well. Spread over the tuna and sprinkle the breadcrumbs over the top. Bake for about 20 minutes, or until the fish is just opaque. Finish off by placing briefly under the hot griller until the breadcrumbs are crisp. Serve with bread to soak up the juices.

Serves 4

Baked Atlantic salmon

16 cherry tomatoes, cut in half
150 g (5½ oz) fresh, ripe pineapple
    flesh, diced
4 x 200 g (7 oz) Atlantic salmon
    fillets, skin on
2 tablespoons balsamic vinegar
2 tablespoons olive oil
100 g (3½ oz) rocket (arugula) or
    baby English spinach
4 tablespoons shredded basil leaves

Fish substitution
    kingfish, large trout fillets,
    blue-eye, cod

Preheat the oven to 180°C (350°F/
Gas 4). Mix the tomatoes and
pineapple together.

Line a baking tray with a piece of foil,
bearing in mind that the foil needs to
be large enough to enclose the four
salmon fillets. Place the salmon fillets
on the foil and season with salt and
pepper. Spoon the tomato and
pineapple mixture on top of the fillets,
dividing it equally. Whisk the balsamic
vinegar and olive oil together in a
small bowl and drizzle over the top.
Wrap the parcel to enclose the fish
and put in the preheated oven for
20–25 minutes, or until the salmon is
opaque but still moist and succulent.

Make a small bed of rocket or spinach
leaves in the centre of each plate.
Lift the salmon fillets out of the foil
and sit on top of the leaves. Spoon
on the pineapple and tomato mixture,
drizzle with the cooking juices and
sprinkle with basil.

Serves 4

Crunchy fish fillets with chive mayo

160 g (²/₃ cup) good-quality
  mayonnaise
2 tablespoons chopped chives
1 tablespoon sweet chilli sauce
75 g (½ cup) cornmeal
4 x 200 g (7 oz) skinless perch fillets
60 ml (¼ cup) oil

Fish substitution
  snapper, John Dory, whiting,
  haddock, cod

For the chive mayo, combine the mayonnaise, chives and chilli sauce in a small bowl. Keep refrigerated until needed.

Put the cornmeal on a plate. Score four diagonal slashes in the skin side of each fish fillet, to prevent the fish curling during cooking. Press both sides of the fillets into the cornmeal to coat thoroughly.

Heat the oil in a frying pan over medium heat. Add the fish and cook for 3 minutes. Turn and cook for another 3 minutes, or until tender and the fish flakes easily when tested with a fork. Remove and drain on crumpled paper towels. Serve with the chive mayo.

Serves 4

Steamed whole snapper with Asian flavours

800 g (1 lb 12 oz) whole snapper,
  scaled and gutted
3 stems of lemon grass
handful of coriander (cilantro) leaves
small knob of fresh ginger, peeled and
  cut into thin matchsticks
1 large garlic clove, peeled and cut
  into thin slivers
2 tablespoons soy sauce
60 ml (¼ cup) oil
1 tablespoon fish sauce
1 small red chilli, deseeded and
  finely chopped

Fish substitution
  coral trout, sea bass

Score the fish with diagonal cuts on both sides. Cut each stem of lemon grass into three and lightly squash each piece with the end of the handle of a large knife. Put half of the lemon grass in the middle of a large piece of foil and lay the fish on top. Put the remaining lemon grass and half of the coriander leaves inside the cavity of the fish.

Mix the ginger, garlic, soy sauce, oil, fish sauce and chilli together. Drizzle the mixture over the fish and scatter with the remaining coriander leaves.

Enclose the fish in the foil and sit in a large bamboo or metal steamer over a pan of simmering water. Steam for 25 minutes, or until the flesh of the fish is opaque and white. Serve with stir-fried Asian greens and rice.

Serves 2

Fish burgers and wedges

500 g (1 lb 2 oz) skinless flake
  fillets
2 tablespoons finely chopped
  parsley
2 tablespoons finely chopped
  dill
2 tablespoons lemon juice
1 tablespoon capers, drained, rinsed
  and chopped
2 gherkins, finely chopped
350 g (12 oz) potatoes, cooked
  and mashed
plain (all-purpose) flour, for dusting
1 tablespoon olive oil
4 hamburger buns, split into halves
lettuce leaves
2 Roma (plum) tomatoes, sliced
tartare sauce, for serving

Crunchy potato wedges
6 potatoes
1 tablespoon oil, plus extra, for
  deep-frying
1/2 teaspoon chicken salt
25 g (1/4 cup) dry breadcrumbs
2 teaspoons chopped chives
1 teaspoon celery salt
1/4 teaspoon garlic powder
1/2 teaspoon chopped rosemary

Fish substitution
  ling, redfish, warehou

Put the fish fillets in a frying pan and add enough water so that the fish is just covered. Slowly heat the water, making sure it doesn't come to the boil. Cover with a lid and cook over low heat until the fish is just cooked through. Drain the fish on crumpled paper towels, then transfer to a bowl and flake the flesh with a fork, removing any bones.

Add the parsley, dill, lemon juice, capers, gherkins and potato to the bowl with the fish, then season with freshly ground black pepper and some salt, and mix well. Divide the mixture into four and shape each portion into a patty. Lightly dust the patties with flour, cover and refrigerate for 1 hour—this will help them stick together during cooking.

While the patties are resting, make the wedges. Preheat the oven to 200°C (400°F/Gas 6). Wash the potatoes, then cut them into wedges, leaving the skin on. Pat the potato wedges dry with paper towels and then toss with the oil so they are all covered. Combine the chicken salt, breadcrumbs, chives, celery salt, garlic powder and rosemary, and then toss with the wedges. Spread the wedges out onto greased baking trays and bake for 40 minutes, or until golden.

Heat the oil in a large non-stick frying pan, add the fish patties and cook for 5–6 minutes on each side, or until well browned and cooked through.

Grill the buns and butter them if you wish. On each base, put some lettuce, tomato, a fish patty and some tartare sauce. Top with the other half of the bun and serve with the hot potato wedges.

Serves 4

Steamed trout with soy, rice wine and ginger

2 x 200–225 g (7–8 oz) rainbow trout, scaled and gutted
60 ml (¼ cup) soy sauce
½ teaspoon sesame oil
1 teaspoon rice vinegar or white wine vinegar
2 teaspoon rice wine or dry sherry
1 tablespoon finely shredded fresh ginger
2 tablespoons chopped coriander (cilantro) leaves
2 spring onions (scallions), finely chopped

Fish substitution
sea bass, bream

Rinse the fish and pat dry with paper towels. Score both sides of each fish three times and place the fish in a shallow ovenproof dish.

Mix together the soy sauce, sesame oil, vinegar, rice wine and ginger. Pour some of the soy sauce mixture inside the fish and then pour the rest on top of the fish.

Place the dish in a large bamboo or metal steamer set over a pan of simmering water. Cover and steam for 15 minutes, or until the flesh of the fish is opaque—lift up one side of each fish and look inside to see if the flesh around the spine is opaque. If not, cook until it is.

Take off the lid and scatter coriander and spring onions over each fish. Serve a fish to each person, along with some rice.

Serves 2

Red emperor poached in coconut milk

1 litre (4 cups) coconut milk
2 teaspoons grated fresh ginger
3 small red chillies, finely chopped
1 tablespoon chopped coriander
   (cilantro) roots and stems
6 red Asian shallots, finely chopped
6 makrut (kaffir) lime leaves, shredded
2 stems of lemon grass, white part
   only, sliced
2 teaspoons grated lime zest
500 ml (2 cups) fish stock
80 ml (1/3 cup) fish sauce
80 ml (1/3 cup) lime juice, strained
4 x 250 g (9 oz) skinless red emperor
   fillets, each fillet cut into three
   equal portions
coriander (cilantro) leaves, for garnish
1 small red chilli, cut in long strips, for
   garnish
2 makrut (kaffir) lime leaves, extra,
   shredded, for garnish

Fish substitution
   coral trout, snapper, Murray cod

Bring the coconut milk to the boil in a saucepan and boil for 3 minutes. Add the ginger, chilli, coriander roots and stems, chopped shallots, lime leaves, lemon grass and lime zest and bring back to the boil. Add the fish stock and fish sauce and simmer for 15 minutes. Pass through a fine strainer and add the lime juice. Taste and add extra fish sauce if necessary.

Heat the sauce in a large frying pan. When the sauce comes to the boil add the fish, then reduce the heat and simmer very gently for 10–15 minutes, or until just cooked through.

Carefully transfer the fish to a serving platter. Serve with some of the liquid and a sprinkling of coriander, chilli and shreds of lime leaf.

Serves 4

Seafood mornay

80 g (2¾ oz) butter
60 g (½ cup) plain (all-purpose) flour
125 ml (½ cup) dry white wine
250 ml (1 cup) thick (double/heavy)
  cream
250 ml (1 cup) milk
125 g (4½ oz) Cheddar cheese, grated
2 tablespoons wholegrain mustard
1 tablespoon horseradish cream
6 spring onions (scallions), chopped
80 g (1 cup) fresh breadcrumbs
1 kg (2 lb 4 oz) skinless monkfish
  fillets, cut into cubes
450 g (1 lb) scallops, cleaned
400 g (14 oz) cooked, peeled small
  prawns (shrimp)

Topping
240 g (3 cups) fresh breadcrumbs
3 tablespoons chopped parsley
60 g (2¼ oz) butter, melted
125 g (4½ oz) Cheddar cheese,
  grated

Fish substitution
  coley, snapper, flathead

Preheat the oven to 180°C (350°F/ Gas 4). Lightly grease a 2 litre (8 cup) ovenproof dish. Melt 60 g (2¼ oz) of the butter in a saucepan over low heat. Stir in the flour until pale and foaming. Remove the pan from the heat and gradually stir in the wine, cream and milk. Return the pan to the heat and stir over high heat until the sauce boils and thickens. Season to taste with salt and pepper. Add the Cheddar, mustard, horseradish, spring onion and breadcrumbs. Mix well and set aside.

Melt the remaining butter in a large pan and add the fish and scallops in batches. Stir over low heat until the seafood starts to change colour. Drain the seafood, add to the sauce with the prawns, then transfer to the greased dish.

For the topping, mix all the ingredients and spread over the seafood. Bake the mornay for 35 minutes, or until the top is golden and the sauce bubbling.

Serves 8–10

Piri piri prawns

125 ml (½ cup) oil
2 teaspoons dried chilli flakes
4 large garlic cloves, crushed
1 kg (2 lb 4 oz) prawns (shrimp),
   peeled and deveined, tails intact
75 g (2½ oz) butter
60 ml (¼ cup) lemon juice

Put the oil, chilli flakes, garlic and
1 teaspoon salt in a large non-metallic
bowl and mix well. Add the prawns
and coat them in the mixture.
Refrigerate for 3 hours, stirring and
turning occasionally.

Preheat the griller (broiler) to very
hot. Put the prawns in a single layer
on a baking tray and brush with the
remaining oil and chilli mixture. Cook
for about 5 minutes, turning once, or
until cooked through.

Meanwhile, melt the butter with the
lemon juice in a small saucepan.
Serve the prawns hot, drizzled with
the lemon juice and butter mixture
and accompanied with rice.

Serves 4

Winter

Tom yum goong

1 tablespoon oil

500 g (1 lb 2 oz) prawns (shrimp),
peeled and deveined, reserving the
heads and shells

2 tablespoons Thai red curry paste
or tom yum paste

2 tablespoons tamarind purée
(see Note)

2 teaspoons ground turmeric

1 teaspoon chopped red chillies

4 makrut (kaffir) lime leaves, shredded

2 tablespoons fish sauce

2 tablespoons lime juice

2 teaspoons grated palm sugar or
soft brown sugar

2 tablespoons coriander (cilantro)
leaves

Heat the oil in a large saucepan or
wok and cook the prawn heads and
shells for 10 minutes over medium
heat, stirring frequently, until the
heads are deep orange in colour.

Add 250 ml (1 cup) water and the
curry paste to the saucepan. Bring
to the boil and cook for 5 minutes,
or until reduced slightly. Add another
2 litres (8 cups) water and simmer
for 20 minutes. Strain, discarding the
shells and heads, and pour the stock
back into the pan.

Add the tamarind, turmeric, chillies
and lime leaves to the saucepan,
bring to the boil and cook for
2 minutes. Add the prawns and cook
for 5 minutes, or until pink. Stir in the
fish sauce, lime juice and sugar. Serve
sprinkled with coriander leaves.

Serves 4–6

Note: If you are unable to find
tamarind purée, you can make your
own by soaking a 225 g (8 oz) packet
of tamarind pulp in 500 ml (2 cups)
boiling water for 1–2 hours, crushing
occasionally. Push through a sieve
and discard the fibres. Alternatively,
use lemon juice.

Tunisian fish soup

60 ml (¼ cup) olive oil
1 onion, chopped
1 celery stalk, chopped
4 garlic cloves, crushed
2 tablespoons tomato paste (purée)
1½ teaspoons ground turmeric
1½ teaspoons ground cumin
2 teaspoons harissa
1 litre (4 cups) fish stock
2 bay leaves
200 g (1 cup) orzo or other small pasta
500 g (1 lb 2 oz) mixed skinless
    snapper and sea bass fillets, cut
    into bite-sized chunks
2 tablespoons chopped mint, plus
    some extra leaves, for garnish
2 tablespoons lemon juice

Fish substitution
    cod, haddock, ocean perch,
    coral trout

Heat the oil in a large saucepan, add the onion and celery and cook for 8–10 minutes, or until softened. Add the garlic and cook for a further minute. Stir in the tomato paste, turmeric, cumin and harissa and cook, stirring constantly, for an extra 30 seconds.

Pour the fish stock into the saucepan and add the bay leaves. Bring the liquid to the boil, then reduce the heat to low and simmer gently for 15 minutes.

Add the orzo to the liquid and cook for 2–3 minutes, or until *al dente*. Drop the chunks of fish into the liquid and poach gently for 3–4 minutes, or until the fish is opaque. Stir in the mint and lemon juice, season to taste with salt, then serve with warm pitta bread. Garnish with mint leaves.

Serves 6

Bourride

Garlic croutons
½ stale baguette, sliced
60 ml (¼ cup) olive oil
1 garlic clove, halved

Aïoli
2 egg yolks
4 garlic cloves, crushed
3–5 teaspoons lemon juice
250 ml (1 cup) olive oil

Stock
¼ teaspoon saffron threads
1 litre (4 cups) dry white wine
1 leek, white part only, chopped
2 carrots, chopped
2 onions, chopped
2 long strips of orange zest
2 teaspoons fennel seeds
3 thyme sprigs

2.5 kg (5½ lb) monkfish fillets,
    skinned and cut into 4 cm
    (1½ inch) pieces, reserving
    the trimmings for use in the stock
3 egg yolks
thyme sprigs, for garnish

Fish substitution
    sea bass, cod, perch, sole, bream

Preheat the oven to 160°C (315°F/ Gas 2–3). To make the croutons, brush the bread with oil and bake for 10 minutes, or until crisp. Rub one side of each slice with garlic.

To make the aïoli, put the egg yolks, garlic and 3 teaspoons of the lemon juice in a mortar and pestle or food processor and pound or mix until light and creamy. Add the oil, drop by drop, whisking constantly until it begins to thicken, then add the oil in a very thin stream. If you're using a food processor, pour in the oil in a thin stream with the motor running. Season with salt and pepper, add the remaining lemon juice and, if necessary, thin with a little warm water. Cover and refrigerate until you're ready to serve.

To make the stock, soak the saffron in a tablespoon of hot water for 15 minutes. Put the saffron and its soaking liquid, the wine, leek, carrot, onion, orange zest, fennel seeds, thyme and fish trimmings in a large saucepan with 1 litre (4 cups) water. Cover and bring to the boil, then simmer for 20 minutes, occasionally skimming the impurities off the surface. Strain the liquid into a clean saucepan, pressing down on the solids with a wooden spoon to extract all the liquid.

Bring the stock to a gentle simmer, add half the pieces of fish and poach for 5 minutes. Remove the fish with a slotted spoon and keep warm while you cook the rest of the fish, then remove all the fish pieces from the pan and bring the stock back to the boil. Boil for 5 minutes, or until slightly reduced, and remove the pan from the heat.

Put half the aïoli and the egg yolks in a large bowl and mix until smooth. Whisk in a ladleful of hot stock, then gradually add five ladlefuls, stirring constantly. Pour back into the pan with the rest of the stock and whisk over low heat for 3–5 minutes, or until the soup is hot and slightly thicker (don't let it boil or it will curdle). Season with salt and pepper.

To serve, put two garlic croutons in each bowl, top with a few pieces of fish and ladle over the hot soup. Garnish with thyme sprigs. You can either serve the remaining aïoli separately or add a dollop to the soup before you serve it.

Serves 4

Goan fish curry

4 cardamom pods
1 teaspoon coriander seeds
2 teaspoons mustard seeds
2 tablespoons shredded coconut
60 ml (¼ cup) oil
1 large onion, chopped
2 garlic cloves, finely chopped
3 small green chillies, deseeded and
  finely chopped
1 tablespoon grated fresh ginger
½ teaspoon ground turmeric
pinch of freshly grated nutmeg
4 cloves
2 tablespoons tamarind purée
6 curry leaves
2 cinnamon sticks
800 ml (28 fl oz) coconut milk
600 g (1 lb 5 oz) skinless pomfret
  fillets, cut into strips
12 small prawns (shrimp), peeled and
  deveined
coriander (cilantro) leaves, for garnish

Fish substitution
  flounder, plaice, sole

Lightly crush the cardamom pods until the pods split, then remove the seeds from the pods and put in a small frying pan with the coriander seeds. Dry-fry until fragrant and the seeds begin to jump. Remove from the heat and tip into a mortar and pestle or spice grinder. Grind the seeds to a powder.

Tip the mustard seeds into the frying pan with the coconut and toast together until the seeds begin to pop and the coconut turns light golden. Remove from the heat and set aside.

Heat the oil in a saucepan and add the onion. Cook for 4–5 minutes, or until it is starting to soften. Add the garlic, chilli, ginger, turmeric and nutmeg and cook for a further minute. Tip in the ground spices, the toasted coconut and mustard seeds, the cloves, tamarind, curry leaves, cinnamon sticks and coconut milk. Stir well and heat to just below boiling point, then reduce the heat and simmer, uncovered, for 10 minutes, or until slightly thickened. Add the strips of fish and the prawns and poach for 5 minutes, or until the fish is opaque and the prawns are pale pink. Garnish with coriander leaves.

Serves 4

Caldeirada

800 g (1 lb 12 oz) waxy potatoes,
  cut into thick slices
60 ml (¼ cup) olive oil
1 large onion, thinly sliced
4 large garlic cloves, finely chopped
1 red capsicum (pepper), sliced
1 tablespoon paprika
1 tablespoon red wine vinegar
100 ml (3½ fl oz) dry white wine
400 g (14 oz) mussels, cleaned
4 x 100 g (3½ oz) hake steaks
12 prawns (shrimp), peeled and
  deveined

Fish substitution
  cod, bream, sea bass

Put the potato in a saucepan, cover with boiling water, then bring to the boil. Reduce the heat to medium, add a pinch of salt and simmer for 10 minutes, or until tender. Drain and arrange in a serving dish, keeping warm in a low oven if necessary.

Meanwhile, heat the oil in a large, wide sauté pan (with a lid), then cook the onion for 5 minutes over medium heat. Add the garlic and capsicum and cook for a minute, stirring. Add the paprika, vinegar, wine and 2½ tablespoons water. Bring to the boil, add the mussels and cover. Allow to bubble for 4 minutes (the mussels should open), then remove the mussels from the pan, discarding any that have not opened, and reduce the heat to low.

Put the fish steaks and prawns on top of the onion mixture, cover and cook for 7 minutes, turning both halfway. Return the mussels to the pan for the final minute to heat through. When cooked the fish will be opaque and the prawns will be pink. Season. Spoon the seafood mixture over the top of the potato, then serve.

Serves 4

Brazilian seafood stew

4 x 200 g (7 oz) bream steaks
200 g (7 oz) large prawns (shrimp),
  peeled and deveined
2½ tablespoons lime juice
2 tablespoons olive oil
1 large onion, finely chopped
4 large garlic cloves, crushed
1 large red capsicum (pepper),
  chopped
1 habanero chilli, deseeded and
  finely chopped
500 g (1 lb 2 oz) ripe tomatoes
300 ml (10½ fl oz) coconut milk
chopped coriander (cilantro) leaves,
  for garnish
thin strips of lime zest, for garnish

Fish substitution
  mahi mahi, halibut, sole, cod, bass

Put the fish and prawns in a shallow non-metallic dish. Drizzle the lime juice over the top, season, then turn the seafood in the juice. Cover and marinate in the fridge for 30 minutes.

Meanwhile, heat the oil in a large saucepan and add the onion. Cook for 8–10 minutes, or until softened, then add the garlic, capsicum and chilli and cook for a further 3 minutes, stirring now and then.

Score a cross in the base of the tomatoes. Soak in boiling water for 30 seconds, then plunge into cold water. Peel the skin away from the cross. Chop the tomatoes, discarding the cores. Add the tomatoes to the pan and cook for 5 minutes, or until the mixture thickens. Allow to cool a little, then tip the mixture into a food processor or blender and blend until smooth. Return the sauce to the pan. Pour in the coconut milk and bring to a gentle simmer. Lift the fish and prawns out of the dish and add to the pan, leaving behind any remaining marinade. Cook for 4 minutes, or until opaque. Season and sprinkle with coriander and lime zest.

Serves 4

Chunky fish soup with bacon and dumplings

2 tablespoons olive oil
1 onion, chopped
1 small red capsicum (pepper), chopped
1 small zucchini (courgette), diced
150 g (5½ oz) smoked bacon, chopped
1 garlic clove, crushed
2 tablespoons paprika
400 g (14 oz) tin chopped tomatoes
400 g (14 oz) tin chickpeas
450 g (1 lb) skinless pike fillet, cut into large pieces
2 tablespoons chopped flat-leaf (Italian) parsley

Dumplings
75 g (2½ oz) self-raising flour
1 egg, lightly beaten
1½ tablespoons milk
2 teaspoons finely chopped marjoram

Fish substitution
  bream, char, trout

Heat the oil in a large saucepan, then add the onion. Cook over low heat for 8–10 minutes, or until softened. Add the capsicum, zucchini, bacon and garlic and cook over medium heat for 5 minutes, stirring now and then.

Meanwhile, make the dumpling mixture by combining the flour, egg, milk and marjoram together in a bowl with a wooden spoon.

Add the paprika, tomato, chickpeas and 800 ml (28 fl oz) water to the vegetables in the saucepan. Bring the liquid to the boil, then reduce the heat to low and simmer gently for 10 minutes, or until thickened slightly. Using two tablespoons to help you form the dumplings, add six rounds of the dumpling mixture to the soup (this should use up all the mixture). Poach for 2 minutes, then slide the pieces of fish into the liquid. Poach for a further 2–3 minutes, or until the fish is cooked. The dumplings and fish should be ready simultaneously. Season to taste, sprinkle with parsley, then serve.

Serves 6

Thai yellow fish curry

Paste

1 tablespoon chopped fresh turmeric,
  or ½ tablespoon ground turmeric
1 teaspoon ground coriander
1 teaspoon ground cumin
3 small yellow or red chillies
1 stem of lemon grass, cut into
  three pieces
small knob of fresh galangal or ginger,
  peeled
1 tablespoon chopped coriander
  (cilantro) root
2 large garlic cloves, peeled
2 red Asian shallots, peeled
1 teaspoon dried shrimp paste

Curry

60 ml (¼ cup) oil
800 ml (28 fl oz) coconut milk
4 makrut (kaffir) lime leaves (optional)
finely grated zest and juice of 1 lime
1 tablespoon fish sauce
1 teaspoon palm sugar or soft brown
  sugar
30 Thai pea eggplants (aubergines)
  (optional) (see Notes)
4 Thai or other baby eggplants
  (aubergines), quartered or
  150 g (5½ oz) regular eggplant
  (aubergine), cut into small chunks
50 g (1¾ oz) bean sprouts, trimmed
12 tiger prawns (shrimp), peeled and
  deveined, tails intact
600 g (1 lb 5 oz oz) skinless lemon
  sole fillets, cut into bite-sized
  chunks
2 tablespoons Thai basil or other basil
  leaves
1 tablespoon coriander (cilantro)
  leaves

Fish substitution

  cod, hapuka, snapper, kingfish,
  grouper

To make the curry paste, put the turmeric, ground coriander, cumin, chillies, lemon grass, galangal, fresh coriander root, garlic, shallots, shrimp paste and 60 ml (¼ cup) water in a small food processor and whiz until it forms a thick paste. Alternatively, if you don't have a food processor, you can chop all the ingredients very finely with a sharp knife or in a mortar and pestle and then mix everything together by hand.

Heat the oil in a large saucepan or wok, then add the curry paste. Cook, stirring often, for 5 minutes, or until fragrant. Pour in the coconut milk, then add the lime leaves, lime zest and juice, fish sauce, sugar, Thai pea eggplant (if using) and other eggplant. Stir well, bring the mixture to the boil, then reduce the heat to low, cover with a lid and simmer for 15 minutes, or until the curry has thickened slightly and the eggplant is cooked.

Remove the lid from the pan and add the bean sprouts, prawns and chunks of fish. Cook for 4–5 minutes, or until the prawns have turned a pale pink and the fish is opaque. Stir in the basil and coriander, add a little salt if you think it needs it, and serve with steamed rice.

Serves 4

Notes: There are many good-quality ready-made curry pastes available in the Asian section of most supermarkets. If you'd prefer to use one of these rather than making your own, use 3–4 tablespoons yellow curry paste and skip the first step.

Pea eggplants are very small and round, not much bigger than a marble. They are sometimes available at Asian grocery stores.

Russian fish soup

50 g (1³/₄ oz) butter
1 large onion, thinly sliced
1 celery stalk, chopped
5 tablespoons plain (all-purpose) flour
2 tablespoons tomato paste (purée)
1 litre (4 cups) fish stock
2 large gherkins, rinsed and chopped
1 tablespoon capers, rinsed and
    squeezed dry
1 bay leaf
¼ teaspoon freshly grated nutmeg
600 g (1 lb 5 oz) mixed carp, perch
    or bream fillets, skinned and cut
    into chunks
2 tablespoons chopped parsley
2 tablespoons chopped dill, plus a
    little extra, for garnish
sour cream, for serving

Fish substitution
    tench, haddock, sea bass

Melt the butter in a large saucepan.
Add the onion and celery and cook
gently over low heat for 7–8 minutes,
or until softened and translucent.
Increase the heat, stir in the flour
and tomato paste and cook, stirring
constantly, for 30 seconds. Pour in
the fish stock and slowly bring to the
boil, stirring frequently.

Reduce the heat to low and add the
gherkins, capers, bay leaf, nutmeg
and chunks of fish. Poach gently for
2–3 minutes, or until the fish is
opaque. Gently stir in the parsley and
dill and season generously with salt
and pepper. Serve each bowlful of
soup topped with a spoonful of sour
cream and a sprinkling of dill.

Serves 4

Penang laksa

800 g (1 lb 12 oz) whole snapper,
   scaled and gutted
3 tablespoons tamarind purée
1 teaspoon soft brown sugar
125 g (4½ oz) thin dried white rice
   noodles
1 tablespoon oil
100 g (3½ oz) piece cucumber,
   peeled and cut into thin batons
2 red Asian shallots, thinly sliced
200 g (7 oz) peeled pineapple, cut
   into small chunks
1 small red chilli, sliced (optional)
25 g (½ bunch) Vietnamese mint,
   small leaves left whole, the rest
   roughly shredded

Curry paste
1 small onion
1 teaspoon chopped fresh turmeric
1 tablespoon grated fresh ginger
2 small red chillies, roughly chopped
1 teaspoon shrimp paste

Fish substitution
   coral trout, red emperor, cod,
   sea bass

Put the whole fish in a large saucepan and cover with cold water. Add 1 teaspoon salt and bring to the boil. Cook for 10 minutes, skimming any scum that rises to the surface. Lift the fish out of the liquid. Drain the liquid, reserving 750 ml (3 cups), then stir in the tamarind and sugar to make tamarind stock. Take the fish off the bone, discarding the head and skin. Flake roughly—you should end up with 375–400 g (13–14 oz) cooked fish.

To make the curry paste, put all the ingredients and 2 tablespoons water in a food processor and briefly whiz into a paste.

Soak the noodles in boiling water for 10 minutes. Drain.

Heat the oil in a large saucepan and, when sizzling, add the curry paste. Cook for 5 minutes, stirring constantly. Pour in the tamarind stock, bring to the boil, then reduce the heat and simmer for 5 minutes. Add the chunks of fish just for long enough to heat them through.

Divide the noodles among four deep bowls. Top with the cucumber, shallots, pineapple, chilli (if using) and mint. Ladle on the soup, then serve.

Serves 4

Creamy garlic seafood

6 raw Balmain bugs or crabs
50 g (1¾ oz) butter
1 onion, finely chopped
5–6 large garlic cloves, finely chopped
125 ml (½ cup) white wine
500 ml (2 cups) cream
1½ tablespoons Dijon mustard
2 teaspoons lemon juice
500 g (1 lb 2 oz) raw prawns (shrimp),
    peeled and deveined, tails intact
500 g (1 lb 2 oz) skinless perch fillets,
    cut into bite-sized cubes
12 scallops, with roe, cleaned
2 tablespoons chopped flat-leaf
    (Italian) parsley

Fish substitution
    perch, ling, bream, tuna, blue-eye

Cut the heads off the bugs, then use scissors to cut down around the sides of the tail so you can flap open the shell. Remove the flesh in one piece.

Melt the butter in a frying pan and cook the onion and garlic over medium heat for 2 minutes, or until the onion is softened. Add the wine to the pan and cook for 4 minutes, or until reduced by half. Stir in the cream, mustard, and lemon juice and simmer for 5–6 minutes, or until reduced to almost half.

Add the prawns and cook for 1 minute, then add the bug meat and cook for another minute, or until opaque. Add the perch and cook for 2 minutes, or until cooked through (the flesh will flake easily when tested with a fork). Finally, add the scallops and cook for 1 minute, until all the seafood is cooked. Remove the pan from the heat and toss the parsley through. Season to taste. Serve with salad and bread.

Serves 6

Japanese prawn, scallop and noodle soup

4 dried shiitake mushrooms
100 g (3½ oz) dried soba or somen
  noodles
10 g (¼ oz) sachet bonito-flavoured
  soup stock
75 g (2½ oz) carrot, cut into thin
  batons
150 g (5½ oz) firm tofu, cut into
  cubes
16 prawns (shrimp), peeled and
  deveined, tails intact
8 scallops, cleaned
2 spring onions (scallions), finely
  chopped
1 tablespoon mirin
shichimi togarashi, for serving (see
  Note)

Fish substitution
  chunks of firm white fish, fish balls

Soak the mushrooms in 300 ml
(10½ fl oz) boiling water for 30 minutes.
Meanwhile, cook the noodles in
a saucepan of boiling water for
2 minutes, or until just tender, then
drain and rinse with cold water. Return
the noodles to the pan and cover.

In a large saucepan, mix the stock
with 1 litre (4 cups) water. Drain the
mushrooms and add the soaking
liquid to the pan. Chop the mushroom
caps, discarding the stalks. Add the
mushrooms and carrot to the pan and
bring the liquid to the boil. Reduce
the heat to a simmer and cook for
5 minutes. Add the tofu, prawns,
scallops, spring onion and mirin to
the pan. Cook at a gentle simmer for
4 minutes, or until the prawns have
turned pink and are cooked and the
scallops are firm and opaque.

Meanwhile pour hot water over the
noodles and swish the noodles
around to separate and warm them.
Drain. Divide the noodles among four
large bowls and pour the soup over
them, dividing the seafood equally.
Serve, offering the shichimi togarashi
as a flavouring to sprinkle on top.

Serves 4

Note: Shichimi togarashi is a
Japanese condiment.

Thai prawn curry

Curry paste
1 small onion, roughly chopped
3 garlic cloves
4 dried red chillies
4 whole black peppercorns
2 tablespoons chopped lemon grass,
  white part only
1 tablespoon chopped coriander
  (cilantro) root
2 teaspoons grated lime zest
2 teaspoons cumin seeds
1 teaspoon sweet paprika
1 teaspoon ground coriander
2 tablespoons oil

1 tablespoon oil
2 tablespoons fish sauce
2 cm (3/4 inch) piece of fresh galangal,
  thinly sliced
4 makrut (kaffir) lime leaves
400 ml (14 fl oz) tin coconut cream
1 kg (2 lb 4 oz) prawns (shrimp),
  peeled and deveined, tails intact
sliced fresh red chillies, for garnish
  (optional)
coriander (cilantro) leaves, for garnish

To make the curry paste, put all the ingredients and 1 teaspoon salt in a small food processor. Whiz until the mixture forms a smooth paste.

Heat the oil in a pan. Add half the curry paste and stir over low heat for 30 seconds. Add the fish sauce, galangal, lime leaves and coconut cream to the pan, and stir until well combined.

Add the prawns to the pan and simmer, uncovered, for 10 minutes, or until the prawns are cooked and the sauce has thickened slightly. Sprinkle with chilli and coriander leaves and serve with steamed rice.

Serves 4

Note: Store the rest of the curry paste for next time.

Caribbean fish soup

2 tomatoes
2 tablespoons oil
4 French shallots, finely chopped
2 celery stalks, chopped
1 large red capsicum (pepper), chopped
1 Scotch bonnet chilli, deseeded and finely chopped (see Note)
1/2 teaspoon ground allspice
1/2 teaspoon freshly grated nutmeg
850 ml (30 fl oz) fish stock
275 g (9 3/4 oz) orange sweet potato, peeled and cut into cubes
60 ml (1/4 cup) lime juice
500 g (1 lb 2 oz) skinless sea bream fillets, cut into chunks

Fish substitution
   sea bass, cod

Score a cross in the base of each tomato. Soak in boiling water for 30 seconds, then plunge into cold water. Drain and peel the skin away from the cross. Chop the tomatoes, discarding the cores, and reserving any juices.

Heat the oil in a large saucepan, then add the shallots, celery, capsicum, chilli, allspice and nutmeg. Cook for 4–5 minutes, or until the vegetables have softened, stirring now and then. Tip in the chopped tomatoes (including their juices) and stock and bring to the boil. Reduce the heat to medium and add the cubes of sweet potato. Season to taste with salt and pepper and cook for about 15 minutes, or until the sweet potato is tender.

Add the lime juice and chunks of fish to the saucepan and poach gently for 4–5 minutes, or until the fish is cooked through. Season to taste, then serve with lots of crusty bread.

Serves 6

Note: Scotch bonnet chillies looks like a mini capsicum (pepper) and can be green, red or orange. They are extremely hot but have a good, slightly acidic flavour.

Creamy cod stew

3 ripe tomatoes
1 tablespoon dried shrimp
60 ml (1/4 cup) oil
1 onion, chopped
1 small green capsicum (pepper),
  chopped
1 small green chilli, finely chopped
3 garlic cloves, crushed
3 tablespoons crunchy peanut butter
400 ml (14 fl oz) coconut milk
100 g (3 1/2 oz) small okra, topped
  and tailed
1/2 teaspoon paprika
600 g (1 lb 5 oz) skinless cod fillet
3 tablespoons coriander (cilantro)
  leaves

Fish substitution
  bream, bass, prawns (shrimp)

Score a cross in the base of each tomato. Soak in boiling water for 30 seconds, then plunge into cold water. Drain and peel the skin away from the cross. Chop the tomatoes, discarding the cores and reserving any juices. Put the dried shrimp in a small bowl, cover with boiling water and leave to soak for 10 minutes, then drain.

Heat the oil in a deep-sided frying pan or sauté pan. Add the onion and capsicum and cook for 5 minutes, stirring occasionally. Add the chilli and garlic and cook for a further 2 minutes. Add the tomatoes and juices, peanut butter, coconut milk, okra, paprika and dried shrimp. Bring the mixture to the boil, then reduce the heat to medium and simmer for 12–15 minutes, or until the okra are tender. Meanwhile, cut the cod into large chunks.

Add the fish to the pan, stir and simmer gently to cook. Test after 3 minutes—if the cod flakes easily, it is ready. Season and scatter the coriander over the top.

Serves 4

Lobster curry with capsicum

2 raw lobster tails (350 g/12 oz each)
1 tablespoon oil
1–2 tablespoons red curry paste
2 stems of lemon grass, white part
  only, finely chopped
1 red capsicum (pepper), roughly
  chopped
6 black dried Chinese dates (see
  Note)
270 ml (approximately 9 fl oz) tin
  coconut milk
1 tablespoon fish sauce
2 teaspoons soft brown sugar
1 teaspoon grated lime zest
6 tablespoons coriander (cilantro)
  leaves, for garnish
lime wedges, for serving

Fish substitution
  prawns (shrimp), Balmain
  bug tails

Cut down the sides of the lobster tails on the underside. Remove the flesh and cut it into 2 cm (¾ inch) slices.

Heat the oil over medium heat in a wok or deep heavy-based frying pan. Add the curry paste and lemon grass and stir for 1 minute. Add the lobster pieces a few at a time and stir-fry each batch for 2 minutes, or until golden and just cooked. Remove from the wok.

Add the chopped capsicum to the wok and stir-fry for 30 seconds. Add the dates and coconut milk, bring to the boil and cook for 5 minutes, or until the dates are plump. Add the fish sauce, brown sugar and lime zest. Return the lobster to the wok and heat through for 2–3 minutes. Garnish with the coriander leaves and serve with lime wedges and steamed jasmine rice.

Serves 4

Note: Asian food stores sell dried Chinese dates, which are sometimes called jujubes.

Manhattan-style seafood chowder

60 g (2¼ oz) butter
3 streaky bacon rashers, chopped
2 onions, chopped
2 garlic cloves, finely chopped
2 celery stalks, sliced
3 potatoes, diced
3 teaspoons chopped thyme
1.25 litres (5 cups) fish stock
1 kg (2 lb 4 oz) baby clams, cleaned
1 tablespoon tomato paste (purée)
400 g (14 oz) tin chopped tomatoes
375 g (13 oz) skinless ling fillets, cut
   into bite-sized pieces
12 large prawns (shrimp), peeled and
   deveined, tails intact
2 tablespoons chopped parsley

Fish substitution
   cod, flake, hake, tinned baby clams

Melt the butter in a large saucepan, then cook the bacon, onion, garlic and celery over low heat, stirring occasionally, for 5 minutes, or until soft but not brown. Add the potato, thyme and 1 litre (4 cups) of the stock to the saucepan and bring to the boil. Reduce the heat and simmer, covered, for 15 minutes.

Pour the remaining stock into another saucepan and bring to the boil. Tip in the clams, cover and cook for about 3–5 minutes, or until they open. Discard any that do not open. Drain the clam liquid through a muslin-lined sieve and add it to the soup mixture. Pull most of the clams out of their shells, leaving a few intact for garnish.

Stir the tomato paste and chopped tomatoes into the soup and bring back to the boil. Add the fish pieces, clams and prawns and simmer over low heat for 3 minutes, or until the seafood is cooked—the prawns should be pink and the fish opaque. Season with salt and pepper, and stir in the parsley. Serve garnished with the clams in their shells.

Serves 4

Laksa lemak

115 g (4 oz) rice noodles

Paste
3 red chillies, deseeded and chopped
2 stems of lemon grass
small knob of fresh ginger, grated
4 red Asian shallots, peeled
3 teaspoons shrimp paste
3 teaspoons ground turmeric

50 g (1^3/$_4$ oz) candlenuts or unsalted
  macadamias (see Note)
1 tablespoon oil
2 x 400 ml (14 fl oz) tins coconut milk
80 ml (1/3 cup) lime juice
115 g (4 oz) bean sprouts, trimmed
20 tiger prawns (shrimp), peeled and
  deveined
16 large scallops, cleaned
5 g (1/4 cup) Vietnamese mint, most
  shredded, the rest left whole for
  garnish
1/2 Lebanese (short) cucumber,
  peeled, thinly sliced

Fish substitution
  any other large prawn, cubes of any
  firm-fleshed white fish

Soak the noodles in a bowl of boiling
water for 10 minutes. Drain.

To make the paste, put all the paste
ingredients, plus a tablespoon of
water, into a food processor and
blend until smooth. Alternatively, finely
chop by hand and mix well.

Put the nuts in a saucepan and
cook over medium heat until golden,
then remove to a plate. Heat the oil
in the same saucepan, then add
the prepared paste and cook over
medium heat for 2 minutes. Stir in the
coconut milk, then simmer gently for
10 minutes, or until it thickens slightly.
Roughly chop the candlenuts.

When the coconut milk mixture is
ready, add the lime juice and three-
quarters of the bean sprouts to the
pan. Season with salt, then bring
back to a simmer, add the prawns
and scallops and cook for about
5 minutes, or until the prawns turn
pink. Add the shredded mint and the
noodles, then mix the whole mint with
the chopped nuts and cucumber.

Ladle into four deep bowls, then
sprinkle with the remaining bean
sprouts, the mint and nut mixture and
the cucumber.

Serves 4

Prawn pot pies

60 g (2¼ oz) butter
1 leek (white part only), thinly sliced
1 garlic clove, finely chopped
1 kg (2 lb 4 oz) prawns (shrimp),
  peeled and deveined, tails intact
1 tablespoon plain (all-purpose) flour
185 ml (¾ cup) chicken or fish stock
125 ml (½ cup) dry white wine
500 ml (2 cups) cream
2 tablespoons lemon juice
1 tablespoon chopped dill
1 tablespoon chopped flat-leaf (Italian)
  parsley
1 teaspoon Dijon mustard
1 sheet frozen puff pastry, just thawed
1 egg, lightly beaten

Preheat the oven to 220°C (425°F/ Gas 7). Melt the butter in a saucepan over low heat. Cook the leek and garlic for 2 minutes, then add the prawns and cook for 1–2 minutes, or until just pink. Remove the prawns with a slotted spoon and set aside.

Stir the flour into the pan and cook for 1 minute. Add the stock and wine, bring to the boil and cook for 10 minutes, or until nearly all the liquid has evaporated. Stir in the cream, bring to the boil, then reduce the heat and simmer for 20 minutes, or until the liquid reduces by half. Stir in the lemon juice, herbs and mustard.

Using half the sauce, pour an even amount into four 250 ml (1 cup) ramekins. Divide the prawns among the ramekins, then top with the remaining sauce.

Cut the pastry into four rounds, slightly larger than the rim of the ramekins. Place the pastry rounds over the prawn mixture and press around the edges. Prick the pastry and brush with beaten egg. Bake for 20 minutes, or until the pastry is crisp and golden. Serve with a salad and bread.

Serves 4

Lobster soup with zucchini and avocado

50 g (1¾ oz) butter
1 garlic clove, crushed
2 French shallots, finely chopped
1 onion, chopped
1 zucchini (courgette), diced
2½ tablespoons dry white wine
400 ml (14 fl oz) fish stock
250 g (9 oz) raw lobster meat, chopped
250 ml (1 cup) thick (double/heavy)
  cream
1 avocado, diced
1 tablespoon chopped coriander
  (cilantro) leaves
1 tablespoon chopped parsley
lemon juice, to serve

Fish substitution
  crayfish, prawns (shrimp)

Melt the butter in a large saucepan. Add the garlic, chopped shallots, onion and zucchini. Cook over medium heat for 8–10 minutes, or until the vegetables are just soft.

Splash in the wine and bring to the boil, keeping on the boil for 3 minutes. Pour in the stock and bring to the boil again. Reduce the heat to low, add the chunks of lobster and simmer for 3–4 minutes, or until the lobster meat is opaque and tinged pink. Gently stir in the cream and season with salt and pepper.

Ladle the soup into four bowls and stir a little of the avocado, coriander and parsley into each one. Squeeze a little lemon juice over the soup before serving.

Serves 4

African fish stew

4 x 200 g (7 oz) kingfish steaks
1 large onion, sliced
1 red capsicum (pepper), thinly sliced
150 ml (5 fl oz) oil
80 ml (1/3 cup) lemon juice
1 teaspoon cayenne pepper
100 ml (3 1/2 fl oz) fish stock

Fish substitution
   butterfish, marlin

Put the fish in a shallow non-metallic dish. Scatter the onion and capsicum over the top. Combine 80 ml (1/3 cup) of the oil with the lemon juice and cayenne pepper, then pour over the fish, cover and leave to marinate for 30 minutes in the fridge.

Lift the onion and capsicum out of the dish and pat dry. Heat 2 tablespoons of the remaining oil in a deep-sided sauté or frying pan, then add the onion and capsicum. Reduce the heat to low and cook gently for 10 minutes to soften, stirring now and then. Meanwhile, lift the fish out of the marinade and pat dry, reserving the marinade.

Transfer the onion and capsicum to a plate and heat the remaining oil in the pan. Sear the fish for 1 minute on each side. Return the onion and capsicum to the pan with the marinade and stock. Bring the liquid to the boil, then reduce the heat to low and cook gently, covered, for 7 minutes, or until the fish is cooked through. Season and serve with the onion and capsicum.

Serves 4

Mild Indian prawn curry

50 g (1¾ oz) ghee
1 onion, finely chopped
2 ripe tomatoes
2 large garlic cloves, finely chopped
½ teaspoon grated fresh ginger
2 small red chillies, deseeded and
   finely chopped
1 teaspoon ground coriander
1 teaspoon ground cumin
1 teaspoon garam masala
pinch of ground turmeric
2 tablespoons tomato paste (purée)
400 ml (14 fl oz) coconut milk
16 king prawns (shrimp), peeled and
   deveined, tails intact
2 tablespoons shredded mint

Fish substitution
   chunks of firm white fish

Melt the ghee in a saucepan and, when hot, add the chopped onion. Cook for 8–10 minutes, or until the onion is softened.

Meanwhile, score a cross in the base of each tomato. Put in boiling water for 30 seconds, then plunge into cold water. Drain, then peel the skin away from the cross. Roughly chop the tomatoes, discarding the cores and seeds and reserving any juices.

Add the garlic, ginger and chilli to the onion and cook for 2 minutes. Stir in the spices and cook for 1 minute. Add the tomatoes and any juices, tomato paste and coconut milk. Bring to just below boiling point and simmer for 10 minutes. Tip in the prawns and cook for 3–5 minutes, or until the prawns have turned pale pink and opaque. Season with salt and stir in the mint. Serve with chapatis or naan bread to soak up the sauce, or with plain boiled basmati rice.

Serves 4

New England clam chowder

1.5 kg (3 lb 5 oz) clams, cleaned
2 teaspoons oil
3 bacon rashers, chopped
1 onion, chopped
1 garlic clove, crushed
750 g (1 lb 10 oz) potatoes, diced
330 ml (1⅓ cups) fish stock
500 ml (2 cups) milk
125 ml (½ cup) cream
3 tablespoons chopped flat-leaf
  (Italian) parsley

Put the clams in a large heavy-based saucepan with 250 ml (1 cup) water, cover and simmer for about 4 minutes, or until they open. Discard any that do not open. Strain the liquid through a muslin-lined sieve and reserve. Pull most of the clams out of their shells, leaving a few intact as a garnish.

Heat the oil in the cleaned saucepan. Add the bacon, onion and garlic and cook, stirring, over medium heat until the onion is soft and the bacon golden. Add the potato and stir well.

Add enough water to the reserved clam liquid to make 330 ml (1⅓ cups) of liquid in total. Pour this and the stock into the saucepan and bring to the boil, then pour in the milk and bring back to the boil. Reduce the heat, cover and simmer for 20 minutes, or until the potato is tender. Uncover and simmer for 10 minutes, or until slightly thickened. Add the cream, clam meat and parsley and season. Heat through gently, but do not allow to boil or it may curdle. Serve in deep bowls with the clams in shells as a garnish.

Serves 4

Bouillabaisse

Rouille
1 small red capsicum (pepper)
1 slice of white bread, crusts removed
1 red chilli
2 garlic cloves
1 egg yolk
80 ml (1/3 cup) olive oil

Soup
2 tablespoons oil
1 fennel bulb, thinly sliced
1 onion, chopped
750 g (1 lb 10 oz) ripe tomatoes
1.25 litres (5 cups) fish stock or water
pinch of saffron threads
bouquet garni (see Note)
5 cm (2 inch) piece of orange zest
1.5 kg (3 lb 5 oz) monkfish fillets,
   cut into bite-sized pieces
18 black mussels, cleaned

Fish substitution
rascasse, sea bass, snapper, red
mullet, John Dory, eel (skin on)

To make the rouille, preheat the griller (broiler). Cut the capsicum in half lengthways, remove the seeds and membrane and place, skin-side up, under the hot griller until the skin blackens and blisters. Alternatively, hold the hold capsicum over the gas flame of your stove until the skin is blackened. Leave to cool before peeling away the skin. Roughly chop the capsicum flesh. Soak the bread in 60 ml (¼ cup) water, then squeeze dry with your hands. Put the capsicum, bread, chilli, garlic and egg yolk in a mortar and pestle or food processor and pound or mix together. Gradually add the oil in a thin stream, pounding or mixing until the rouille is smooth and has the texture of thick mayonnaise. Cover and refrigerate the rouille until needed.

Heat the oil in a large saucepan and cook the fennel and onion for 5 minutes, or until golden.

Meanwhile, score a cross in the base of each tomato. Cover with boiling water for 30 seconds, then plunge into cold water. Drain and peel the skin away from the cross. Chop the tomatoes, discarding the cores. Add the chopped tomato to the saucepan and cook for 3 minutes. Stir in the stock, saffron, bouquet garni and orange zest, bring to the boil

and boil for 10 minutes. Remove the bouquet garni and orange zest and either push the soup through a sieve or purée in a blender. Return to the cleaned saucepan, season well and bring back to the boil. Reduce the heat to a simmer and add the fish and mussels. Cook for 5 minutes, or until the fish is tender and the mussels have opened. Throw away any mussels that haven't opened in this time. Serve the soup with rouille and bread or toast.

Serves 6

Note: A bouquet garni is used for flavouring soups and stews. You can buy dried ones in the supermarket (look near the rest of the herbs) or make your own by wrapping the green part of a leek around a bay leaf, a sprig of thyme, a sprig of parsley and celery leaves. Tie the bundle with kitchen string.

Fish molee

1 tablespoon oil
1 large onion, thinly sliced
3 garlic cloves, crushed
1–2 small green chillies, finely
  chopped
2 teaspoons ground turmeric
1 teaspoon ground coriander
1 teaspoon ground cumin
4 cloves
6 curry leaves, plus another
  6 for garnish
800 ml (28 fl oz) coconut milk
500 g (1 lb 2 oz) skinless pomfret
  fillets
1 tablespoon chopped fresh coriander
  (cilantro) leaves

Fish substitution
  flounder, sole, plaice, Pacific Dory

Heat the oil in a deep frying pan or sauté pan and cook the onion for 5 minutes. Add the garlic and chilli and cook for a further 5 minutes, or until the onion has softened and looks translucent. Add the turmeric, ground coriander, cumin and cloves and stir-fry with the onion for about 2 minutes before stirring in the curry leaves, coconut milk and 1/2 teaspoon salt. Bring to just below boiling point. Reduce the heat to medium and simmer, without a lid, for 20 minutes, or until slightly thickened.

Cut each fish fillet into two or three large pieces across the fillet. Add the fish to the sauce and bring the sauce back to a simmer, cook for 5 minutes or until the fish is opaque and looks flaky. Season with a little more salt if necessary, then stir in the fresh coriander. Serve garnished with curry leaves. Serve with boiled rice to soak up the sauce.

Serves 4

Gumbo

Roux
80 ml (1/3 cup) oil
75 g (scant 2/3 cup) plain
  (all-purpose) flour
1 onion, finely chopped
1.5 litres (6 cups) boiling water

4 crabs, cleaned
450 g (1 lb) chorizo sausage, cut into
  bite-sized pieces
6 spring onions (scallions), sliced
1 green capsicum (pepper), roughly
  chopped
3 tablespoons chopped parsley
1/4 teaspoon chilli powder
500 g (1 lb 2 oz) prawns (shrimp),
  peeled and deveined
24 oysters, shucked
1/2 teaspoon filé powder (see Note)
1 1/2 tablespoons long-grain rice

To make the roux, pour the oil into a large heavy-based saucepan on low heat. Gradually add the flour, stirring after each addition, to make a thin roux. Continue to cook and stir over a low heat for 35 minutes, or until it turns dark brown. Add the onion and cook for 4 minutes, or until tender. Gradually pour in the boiling water, continually stirring to dissolve the roux, and bring to a simmer.

Cut the crabs into small pieces. Add the crab, sausage, spring onion, capsicum, parsley and chilli powder to the roux. Cook for 30 minutes, then add the prawns and the oysters and their juices and cook for another 5 minutes, or until the prawns are pink. Season well with salt and pepper, then stir in the filé powder.

Meanwhile, cook the rice in salted boiling water for about 10 minutes, or until it is just cooked through. Ladle the gumbo into bowls, each containing a couple of tablespoons of rice in the bottom.

Serves 6

Note: Filé powder is a flavouring often used in Creole cooking. It is made by drying, then grinding sassafras leaves.

Fish smothered with curry sauce

80 ml (⅓ cup) oil
600 g (1 lb 5 oz) skinless pomfret
  fillets
2 large garlic cloves, crushed
4 tablespoons red curry paste
270 ml (approximately 9 fl oz) tin
  coconut milk
80 ml (⅓ cup) fish sauce
2 tablespoons sugar
2 teaspoons lemon juice
2 teaspoons makrut (kaffir) lime
  leaves, finely shredded,
  or 2 teaspoons lime zest
2 tablespoons chopped coriander
  (cilantro) leaves, plus whole leaves,
  for garnish

Fish substitution
  flounder, sole, plaice, blue eye,
  prawns (shrimp)

Heat 2 tablespoons of the oil in a wok or sauté pan until hot. Add the fish, in batches if necessary, and cook for 2–3 minutes, or until opaque. Transfer to a plate and cover with foil.

Wipe out the inside of the wok with paper towels and add the remaining 2 tablespoons of oil. Heat the oil until hot, then add the garlic and curry paste and fry for 30 seconds. Pour in the coconut milk and mix. Add the fish sauce, sugar and lemon juice and heat through. Stir in the shredded lime leaves and chopped coriander and spoon the curry sauce over the fish. Garnish with coriander leaves.

Serves 4

Hearty seafood soup

2 tablespoons dried shrimp
60 ml (¼ cup) olive oil
1 large onion, finely chopped
3 garlic cloves, crushed
1 small red chilli, deseeded and
   finely chopped
1 teaspoon finely grated fresh ginger
3 tablespoons crunchy peanut butter
800 g (1 lb 12 oz) tinned chopped
   tomatoes
50 g (1¾ oz) creamed coconut,
   chopped (see Note)
400 ml (14 fl oz) coconut milk
generous pinch of ground cloves
4 tablespoons chopped coriander
   (cilantro) leaves
700 g (1 lb 9 oz) swordfish, cut into
   large chunks
100 g (3½ oz) small prawns (shrimp),
   peeled and deveined
2 tablespoons chopped cashew nuts

Fish substitution

   marlin, tuna, monkfish

Soak the dried shrimp in boiling water
for 10 minutes, then drain.

Heat the oil in a deep saucepan and
cook the onion gently for 5 minutes.
Add the garlic, chilli and ginger and
cook for 2 minutes. Stir in the dried
shrimp, peanut butter, tomato,
creamed coconut, coconut milk,
ground cloves and half of the
coriander. Bring the mixture to the boil
and simmer gently for 10 minutes.

Remove from the heat, allow to cool a
little, then tip the sauce into a food
processor or blender and blend until
thick and smooth. Alternatively, push
the mixture through a coarse sieve or
mouli by hand.

Return the sauce to the pan over
medium heat. Add the swordfish and
cook for 2 minutes, then add the
prawns and continue to simmer until
all the seafood is cooked—the prawns
will be pink and the fish opaque. Serve
with the cashews and remaining
coriander sprinkled over the top.

Serves 4

Note: Creamed coconut is sold in
a block. It needs to be chopped or
grated and then stirred into a hot
liquid. If you can't find it, use a 140 g
(5 oz) tin of thick coconut cream.

Mexican soup with salsa

60 ml (¼ cup) olive oil
1 large onion, chopped
1 large celery stalk, chopped
3 garlic cloves, crushed
2 small thin red chillies, deseeded
  and finely chopped
200 ml (7 fl oz) fish stock
800 g (1 lb 12 oz) tinned chopped
  tomatoes
2 bay leaves
1 teaspoon dried oregano
1 teaspoon caster (superfine) sugar
2 large cobs of corn, kernels removed
500 g (1 lb 2 oz) halibut fillets, skinned
2 tablespoons chopped coriander
  (cilantro) leaves
juice of 2 limes
12 prawns (shrimp), peeled and
  deveined, tails intact
8 scallops, cleaned
12 clams, cleaned
125 g (½ cup) thick (double/heavy)
  cream

Salsa
½ small avocado
1 tablespoon coriander (cilantro)
  leaves
finely grated zest and juice of 1 lime
½ small red onion, finely chopped

Fish substitution
  swordfish, kingfish, snapper

Heat the oil in a large saucepan. Add the onion and celery and cook over medium heat for 10 minutes, stirring now and then. Add the garlic and chilli to the pan and cook for 1 minute, stirring. Add the fish stock and tomatoes and break up the tomatoes in the pan using a wooden spoon.

Stir in the bay leaves, oregano and sugar and bring to the boil. Allow to bubble for 2 minutes, then reduce the heat to low and gently simmer for 10 minutes. Cool for 5 minutes, remove the bay leaves, then tip the tomato mixture into a food processor or blender and whiz until fairly smooth, but not completely so. Alternatively, push the mixture through a coarse sieve or mouli by hand.

Return the tomato sauce to the saucepan and season with salt. Add the corn kernels and bring back to the boil. Reduce the heat to a simmer to cook for 3 minutes, or until the kernels are just tender. Cut the fish into large chunks.

Stir the coriander and the lime juice into the sauce, add the fish to the pan, then simmer gently for a minute. Add the prawns and scallops and scatter the clams on the top. Cover with a lid and cook gently for a further 2–3 minutes, or until the seafood is

opaque and cooked through, the prawns have turned pink and the clams have steamed open. Discard any clams that have not opened by now.

While the fish is poaching, make the salsa. Chop the avocado into small cubes and mix with the coriander, the lime zest and juice, and red onion and season with salt and pepper. Before serving, stir the cream into the soup, ladle into deep bowls and top with salsa. Serve with sourdough.

Serves 4

Hot and sour fish stew

Spice paste
2 stems of lemon grass, white part
   only, each cut into three pieces
1 teaspoon ground turmeric
small knob of fresh galangal or ginger
3 small red chillies
1 large garlic clove, peeled
4 red Asian shallots, peeled
1 teaspoon shrimp paste

60 ml (¼ cup) oil
½ small red capsicum (pepper),
   thinly sliced
3 tablespoons tamarind purée or
   lemon juice
1 tablespoon fish sauce
2 teaspoons palm sugar or
   soft brown sugar
225 g (8 oz) tin sliced bamboo
   shoots, drained
500 g (1 lb 2 oz) skinless pomfret
   fillets, cut into bite-sized pieces
2 tablespoons chopped coriander
   (cilantro) leaves
1 tablespoon chopped mint

Fish substitution
   lemon sole (lemon fish), plaice,
   sea bass, flounder, John Dory

To make the spice paste, put all the
ingredients in a food processor and
process to a paste. Alternatively, finely
chop all the ingredients and mix
together by hand.

Heat the oil in a large saucepan, then
add the paste. Cook for 10 minutes,
stirring. Add the strips of capsicum
and cook for a further minute. Pour in
750 ml (3 cups) water, the tamarind,
fish sauce, sugar and ½ teaspoon
salt and bring to the boil. Reduce the
heat to low and simmer for 5 minutes,
then add the bamboo shoots and fish
pieces and poach the fish gently for
3–4 minutes, or until opaque. Stir in
the coriander and mint and serve with
plenty of rice.

Serves 4

Creamy clam soup

1.75 kg (4 lb) clams, cleaned
50 g (1³/₄ oz) butter
1 onion, chopped
1 celery stalk, chopped
1 large carrot, chopped
1 large leek, sliced into rings
250 g (9 oz) swede (rutabaga), diced
800 ml–1 litre (28–35 fl oz) fish stock
1 bay leaf
75 g (heaped ¹/₃ cup) medium- or
   short-grain rice
200 ml (7 fl oz) cream
3 tablespoons finely chopped parsley

Fish substitution
   pipis

Put the clams and 250 ml (1 cup) water in a large saucepan. Bring to the boil, then reduce the heat to medium and cover with a tight-fitting lid. Cook for 3–4 minutes, or until the shells open. Strain into a bowl. Add enough stock to make up to 1 litre (4 cups). Discard any clams that haven't opened by now. Remove all but eight of the clams from their shells.

Melt the butter in a clean saucepan. Add the vegetables and cook, covered, over medium heat for 10 minutes, stirring now and then. Add the stock and bay leaf, bring to the boil, then reduce the heat and simmer for 10 minutes. Add the rice, bring back to the boil, cover and cook over medium heat for 15 minutes, or until the rice and vegetables are tender. Take off the heat and stir in the clam meat. Remove the bay leaf and allow to cool for 10 minutes.

Purée the soup in a blender until smooth, then return to a clean saucepan. Stir in the cream and season. Gently reheat the soup. Add the parsley and two clams in the shell to each bowl.

Serves 4

Malaysian fish curry

3–6 red chillies, roughly chopped,
  plus extra sliced chillies, for garnish
1 onion, chopped
4 garlic cloves, peeled
3 stems of lemon grass, white part
  only, sliced
4 cm (1 1/2 inch) piece of fresh ginger,
  sliced
2 teaspoons shrimp paste
60 ml (1/4 cup) oil
1 tablespoon fish curry powder
  (see Note)
250 ml (1 cup) coconut milk
1 tablespoon tamarind concentrate
1 tablespoon kecap manis
500 g (1 lb 2 oz) skinless ling fillets,
  cut into cubes
2 ripe tomatoes, chopped
1 tablespoon lemon juice

Fish substitution
  flake, hake, coley

Combine the chillies, onion, garlic, lemon grass, ginger and shrimp paste in a small food processor and process until roughly chopped. Add 2 tablespoons of the oil and process until the mixture forms a smooth paste, regularly scraping down the side of the bowl with a spatula.

Heat the remaining oil in a wok or deep heavy-based frying pan and add the paste. Cook for 3–4 minutes over low heat, stirring constantly until very fragrant. Add the curry powder and stir for another 2 minutes. Add the coconut milk, tamarind, kecap manis and 250 ml (1 cup) water to the wok. Bring to the boil, stirring occasionally, then reduce the heat and simmer for 10 minutes, or until slightly thickened.

Add the fish, tomato and lemon juice. Season to taste. Simmer for 5 minutes, or until the fish is just cooked. Serve with rice.

Serves 4

Note: Fish curry powder is a special blend of spices suited to seafood flavours. It is available from Asian food stores.

Cioppino

2 whole crabs
60 ml (¼ cup) olive oil
1 large onion, finely chopped
1 carrot, finely chopped
2–3 garlic cloves, crushed
1 red chilli, finely chopped
400 g (14 oz) tin chopped tomatoes
1 tablespoon tomato paste (purée)
250 ml (1 cup) red wine
500 ml (2 cups) fish stock
1 sprig of thyme
2 sprigs of parsley
375 g (13 oz) prawns (shrimp),
    peeled and deveined
1 kg (2 lb 4 oz) skinless mixed hake,
    snapper or monkfish fillets, cut into
    bite-sized pieces
12–15 mussels, cleaned
1 tablespoon chopped parsley, extra
1 tablespoon chopped basil

Pull the apron back from underneath the crab and separate the shells. Remove the feathery gills and intestines. Twist off the claws. Using a cleaver or large knife, cut the crabs into quarters. Crack the claws either with crab crackers or the back of a heavy knife.

Heat the oil in a large heavy-based saucepan, add the onion, carrot, garlic and chilli and stir over medium heat for about 5 minutes, or until the onion is soft. Add the tomatoes, tomato paste, wine, stock, thyme and parsley sprigs. Bring to the boil, reduce the heat, then cover and simmer for 30 minutes.

Add the crab pieces to the broth and simmer for 5 minutes, then add the prawns and simmer for 1 minute. Add the fish pieces and mussels and simmer for another 2–3 minutes, or until the fish pieces are opaque. Season well. Discard any unopened mussels. Sprinkle with parsley and basil. Serve, making sure you have finger bowls on the table.

Serves 4

Summer

Warm prawn, rocket and feta salad

4 spring onions (scallions), chopped
4 Roma (plum) tomatoes, chopped
1 red capsicum (pepper), chopped
400 g (14 oz) tin chickpeas, drained
1 tablespoon chopped dill
3 tablespoons finely shredded basil
60 ml (¼ cup) extra virgin olive oil
60 g (2¼ oz) butter
1 kg (2 lb 4 oz) prawns (shrimp),
  peeled and deveined, tails intact
2 small red chillies, finely chopped
4 garlic cloves, crushed
2 tablespoons lemon juice
300 g (2 bunches) rocket (arugula)
150 g (5½ oz) feta cheese

Put the spring onion, tomato, capsicum, chickpeas, dill and shredded basil in a large bowl and toss together well.

Heat the oil and butter in a large frying pan or wok, add the prawns and cook, stirring, over high heat for 3 minutes. Add the chilli and garlic and continue cooking for 2 minutes, or until the prawns turn pink. Remove the pan from the heat and stir in the lemon juice.

Arrange the rocket leaves on a large serving platter, top with the tomato and chickpea mixture, then the prawn mixture. Crumble the feta cheese over the top, then serve.

Serves 6

Barbecued salmon cutlets with sweet cucumber dressing

2 small Lebanese (short) cucumbers, peeled, deseeded and finely diced
1 red onion, finely chopped
1 red chilli, finely chopped
2 tablespoons pickled ginger, shredded
2 tablespoons rice vinegar
1/2 teaspoon sesame oil
4 salmon cutlets
1 sheet toasted nori (dried seaweed), cut into thin strips

Fish substitution
ocean trout cutlets

Combine the cucumber, onion, chilli, ginger, rice vinegar and sesame oil in a bowl, cover and stand at room temperature while you cook the salmon cutlets.

Preheat a barbecue flatplate and lightly brush it with oil. Cook the salmon on the barbecue for about 2 minutes on each side, or until cooked as desired. Be careful you do not overcook the fish or it will be dry—it should be still just pink in the centre. Serve the salmon topped with the cucumber dressing, then sprinkle with strips of toasted nori. Serve with steamed rice.

Serves 4

Barbecued fish with onions and ginger

1 kg (2 lb 4 oz) small, firm whole
    snapper, scaled and gutted
2 teaspoons green peppercorns,
    drained and finely crushed
2 teaspoons finely chopped red
    chillies
3 teaspoons fish sauce
60 ml (¼ cup) oil
2 onions, thinly sliced
4 cm (1½ inch) piece of fresh ginger,
    thinly sliced
3 garlic cloves, cut into very thin
    slivers
2 teaspoons sugar
4 spring onions (scallions), finely
    shredded

Lemon and garlic sauce
60 ml (¼ cup) lemon juice
2 tablespoons fish sauce
1 tablespoon sugar
2 small red chillies, finely chopped
3 garlic cloves, chopped

Fish substitution
    bream, red emperor

Wash the fish and pat dry inside and out. Cut two or three diagonal slashes into the thickest part on both sides.

Mix the peppercorns, chillies and fish sauce to a paste and brush over the fish. Refrigerate for 20 minutes.

Meanwhile, to make the lemon and garlic sauce, stir the lemon juice, fish sauce, sugar, chilli and garlic in a bowl until the sugar has dissolved.

Heat a barbecue flatplate until very hot and brush with 1 tablespoon of oil. Cook the fish for 8 minutes on each side, or until the flesh flakes easily when tested with a fork.

While the fish is cooking, heat the remaining oil in a pan and stir the onion over medium heat for a few minutes, or until golden. Add the ginger, garlic and sugar and cook for another 3 minutes. Serve over the fish. Sprinkle with spring onion and serve with the sauce and steamed rice to soak up the sauce.

Serves 4

Herbed bugs with sweet cider sauce

16 Balmain bugs
80 ml (1/3 cup) olive oil
150 ml (5 fl oz) lemon juice
3 garlic cloves, crushed
15 g (1/2 cup) finely chopped flat-leaf
  (Italian) parsley
3 tablespoons finely chopped dill,
  plus some extra, for garnish
80 ml (1/3 cup) apple cider
40 g (1 1/2 oz) butter
crusty bread, for serving
mixed salad, for serving

Fish substitution
  scampi

Remove the heads from the bugs, then cut them in half lengthways. Place in a single layer in a shallow non-metallic dish. Combine the olive oil, lemon juice, garlic, parsley and dill, and pour over the bugs. Cover and refrigerate for at least 1 hour.

Cook the bugs on a chargrill pan (griddle) or barbecue flatplate, shell-side down, for 2 minutes. Turn and cook for another 2 minutes, or until tender. Transfer to a serving platter.

Simmer the apple cider in a small saucepan until reduced by two-thirds. Reduce the heat and add the butter, stirring until melted. Remove from the heat, pour over the bugs and serve. Serve with crusty bread and a green salad.

Serves 4

Swordfish shish kebabs with herb yoghurt and couscous

800 g (1 lb 12 oz) skinless swordfish
  fillet, cut into 3 cm (1¼ inch) chunks
80 ml (⅓ cup) lemon juice
80 ml (⅓ cup) olive oil
3 bay leaves
16 whole cherry tomatoes or 2 firm
  tomatoes, each cut into 8 wedges
2 small red onions, each cut into
  8 wedges
2 small red or orange capsicums
  (peppers), each deseeded and cut
  into 8 chunks

Lemon and herb yoghurt
200 g (7 oz) Greek-style yoghurt
3 teaspoons lemon juice
pinch of paprika
1 tablespoon finely chopped mint
1 tablespoon finely chopped parsley

Couscous
400 g (14 oz) instant couscous
400 ml (14 fl oz) boiling stock
1 tablespoon olive oil
30 g (1 oz) butter

Fish substitution
  tuna, marlin, flake, kingfish,
  barramundi

Put the chunks of swordfish in a non-metallic bowl with the lemon juice, olive oil and bay leaves. Toss to mix, cover and leave to marinate for at least 2 hours in the fridge.

In a small bowl, whisk together the ingredients for the Lemon and herb yoghurt. Refrigerate until needed.

Thread five chunks of fish, two cherry tomatoes, two pieces of onion and two pieces of capsicum onto a metal skewer, alternating between the fish and the various vegetables as you go. You'll need eight skewers in total.

Cook the kebabs on a chargrill pan or barbecue flatplate for 8–10 minutes. Baste with the remaining marinade as they cook, and turn every now and then. When ready the fish should be firm and opaque and the vegetables slightly charred.

Meanwhile, tip the couscous into a heatproof bowl, pour on the stock and oil, cover tightly and leave to sit for 5 minutes. Fluff the grains with a fork and stir in the butter.

Serve the kebabs on a mound of couscous, drizzled with some of the yoghurt dressing.

Serves 4

Caesar salad with sardines

Dressing
1 egg
2 garlic cloves
2 tablespoons lemon juice
1/2 teaspoon Worcestershire sauce
3–4 anchovy fillets
125 ml (1/2 cup) extra virgin olive oil

100 g (1 cup) dry breadcrumbs
65 g (2/3 cup) grated Parmesan
   cheese
2 tablespoons chopped fresh parsley
2 eggs, lightly beaten
80 ml (1/3 cup) milk
16 sardines, scaled and butterflied
oil, for deep-frying
12 small pappadoms
1 baby cos lettuce, leaves separated
8 slices of prosciutto, cooked
   until crisp
50 g (1/2 cup) shaved Parmesan
   cheese

Fish substitution
   small herring, mackerel

To make the dressing, put the egg in a food processor, add the garlic, lemon juice, Worcestershire sauce and anchovies and process to combine. With the motor running, add the oil in a thin, steady stream until the dressing has thickened slightly. Set aside until you're ready to serve.

Put the breadcrumbs, grated Parmesan and parsley in a bowl and mix well. Put the beaten eggs and milk in another bowl and whisk well. Dip the sardines into the egg wash, then into the crumb mixture, and put on a paper-lined baking tray. Refrigerate for an hour.

Heat the oil in a deep-fat fryer or heavy-based frying pan until 180°C (350°F), or until a small cube of white bread dropped into the oil browns in 15 seconds. Deep-fry the pappadoms until crisp, then drain on paper towels. Deep-fry the sardines in batches until crisp and golden.

Arrange the lettuce on a plate, top with prosciutto, sardines, pappadoms and Parmesan, then drizzle with the dressing.

Serves 4

Cajun swordfish

1 tablespoon garlic powder
1 tablespoon onion powder
2 teaspoons white pepper
2 teaspoons cracked black pepper
2 teaspoons dried thyme
2 teaspoons dried oregano
1 teaspoon cayenne pepper
4 swordfish steaks
oil, for cooking
lime wedges, for serving
Greek-style yoghurt, for serving
mixed salad leaves, for serving

Fish substitution
tuna, mahi mahi, kingfish,
striped marlin

Mix all the dried spices and herbs in a bowl. Pat the swordfish steaks dry with paper towels, then coat both sides of each steak in the spice mixture, shaking off any excess.

Heat a barbecue flatplate and drizzle with a little oil. Cook the swordfish steaks for 3–5 minutes on each side, depending on the thickness of each steak. Serve with wedges of lime, a dollop of yoghurt and a salad.

Serves 4

Rosemary tuna kebabs

3 tomatoes
1 tablespoon olive oil
2–3 small red chillies, deseeded
  and chopped
3–4 garlic cloves, crushed
1 red onion, finely chopped
60 ml (¼ cup) white wine or water
400 g (14 oz) tin chickpeas
3 tablespoons chopped oregano
4 tablespoons chopped parsley
lemon wedges, for serving

Tuna kebabs
1 kg (2 lb 4 oz) piece of tuna, cut into
  4 cm (1½ inch) cubes
8 stems of rosemary, about 20 cm
  (8 inches) long, with the leaves from
  the stem thinned out a little
cooking oil spray

Fish substitution
  swordfish, striped marlin, salmon

Cut the tomatoes into halves or quarters and use a teaspoon to scrape out the seeds. Roughly chop the flesh.

Heat the oil in a large non-stick frying pan. Add the chilli, garlic and red onion and stir over medium heat for 5 minutes, or until softened. Add the chopped tomato and the white wine or water. Cook over low heat for 10 minutes, or until the mixture is soft and pulpy and most of the liquid has evaporated. Stir in the rinsed chickpeas with the oregano and parsley. Season to taste with salt and freshly ground black pepper.

Heat a griller (broiler) or barbecue flatplate. Thread the tuna onto the rosemary stems, lightly spray with oil, then cook, turning, for 3 minutes, or until lightly browned on the outside but still a little pink in the centre. Serve with the chickpeas and some lemon wedges.

Serves 4

Redfish in corn husks with asparagus and red capsicum salad

Salad
1 red capsicum (pepper)
2 tablespoons virgin olive oil
1 small garlic clove, crushed
1 tablespoon lemon juice
1 tablespoon chopped basil
1 tablespoon pine nuts
100 g (½ cup) small black olives

6 small red mullet, scaled and gutted
12 sprigs of lemon thyme
1 lemon, sliced
2 garlic cloves, sliced
12 large corn husks
olive oil, for drizzling
2 bunches of fresh asparagus, trimmed
lemon wedges, for serving

Fish substitution
  red mullet

To make the salad, cut the capsicum into large pieces. Put skin-side up under a hot griller (broiler) until the skin blackens and blisters. Alternatively, hold over the coals or gas flame of a barbecue. Cool in a plastic bag, then peel off the skin. Finely dice the flesh.

Combine the olive oil, garlic, lemon juice and basil in a small bowl and whisk together. Add the capsicum, pine nuts and olives.

Wash the fish and pat dry inside and out with paper towels. Fill each fish cavity with thyme, lemon and garlic, then place each in a corn husk. Drizzle with oil and sprinkle with pepper, then top each fish with another husk. Tie each end of the husks with string to enclose.

Place on coals or on a barbecue and cook, turning once, for 6–8 minutes, or until the fish is cooked and flakes easily when tested with a fork. A few minutes after you've started cooking the fish, brush the asparagus with oil and cook, turning occasionally, on the barbecue for 3–4 minutes, or until tender. Pour the dressing over the asparagus and serve with the fish and salad.

Serves 6

Lemon and herb rainbow trout

3 tablespoons chopped dill
2 tablespoons chopped rosemary
4 tablespoons roughly chopped
  flat-leaf (Italian) parsley
2 teaspoons thyme
1½ tablespoons green peppercorns,
  drained and crushed
80 ml (⅓ cup) lemon juice
1 lemon, sliced, plus some extra
  slices, for garnish (optional)
4 whole rainbow trout, scaled and
  gutted
80 ml (⅓ cup) dry white wine

Horseradish cream
1 tablespoon horseradish cream
125 g (½ cup) sour cream
2 tablespoons cream

Lemon sauce
150 g (5½ oz) butter
2 egg yolks
3–4 tablespoons lemon juice

Fish substitution
  baby salmon, Atlantic salmon
  steaks

Cut eight sheets of foil large enough to wrap the fish in. Lay four of them out on a flat surface, then put a second sheet on each piece so that each piece is a double thickness. Lightly grease the top sheets.

Heat a barbecue. Mix the herbs, peppercorns, juice and salt and freshly ground black pepper, to taste, in a bowl. Put a few slices of lemon in each fish cavity. Wipe any slime off the fish with paper towel. Spoon the herb mixture into the fish cavities. Lay each fish onto a piece of foil and sprinkle each with 1 tablespoon of wine. Fold the foil to form parcels. Cook on the barbecue for about 15 minutes, or until the fish is just cooked through. If you like, cook some extra lemon slices on the barbecue to use as a garnish.

Leave the wrapped fish for 5 minutes, then serve with horseradish cream and lemon sauce.

For the horseradish cream, mix the creams in a bowl and season with salt and pepper, to taste.

For the lemon sauce, melt the butter in a small saucepan over low heat, without stirring. Skim the foam off the surface and pour off the clear yellow liquid, leaving the milky sediment behind. Discard the sediment. Blend the egg yolks in a food processor for 20 seconds. With the motor running, add the butter slowly in a thin, steady stream. Continue processing until all the butter has been added and the mixture is thick and creamy. Add the lemon juice and season with salt and pepper. Garnish the fish with barbecued lemon slices and perhaps some strips of chives.

Serves 4

Note: If you are using Atlantic salmon steaks, place the salmon on a bed of the lemon slices and spread the herb mixture over the top, or cut a slit through the centre of the steak and fill with the lemon and herb mixture.

Smoked tuna and white bean salad with basil dressing

100 g (2 handfuls) rocket (arugula)
1 small red capsicum (pepper), cut into julienne strips
1 small red onion, chopped
310 g (11 oz) tin cannellini beans, drained and rinsed
125 g (4½ oz) cherry tomatoes, cut into halves
2 tablespoons capers, rinsed and squeezed dry
2 x 125 g (4½ oz) tins smoked tuna slices in oil, drained

Basil dressing
1 tablespoon lemon juice
1 tablespoon white wine
60 ml (¼ cup) extra virgin olive oil
1 garlic clove, crushed
2 tablespoons chopped basil
½ teaspoon sugar

fish substitution
fresh tuna, seared on both sides, then sliced, or tinned salmon or tuna

Trim any long stems from the rocket, rinse, pat dry and divide among four serving plates.

Lightly toss the capsicum in a large bowl with the onion, beans, tomatoes and capers. Spoon some onto each plate, over the rocket, then scatter tuna over each.

For the dressing, thoroughly whisk all the ingredients in a bowl with 1 tablespoon of water, ¼ teaspoon of salt and freshly ground black pepper, to taste. Drizzle over the salad and serve with bread.

Serves 4

Fish tikka

Marinade
500 g (2 cups) Greek-style yoghurt
2 red Asian shallots, finely chopped
1 tablespoon grated fresh ginger
2 garlic cloves, crushed
2 tablespoons lemon juice
1 teaspoon ground coriander
1 tablespoon garam masala
1 teaspoon paprika
1 teaspoon chilli powder
2 tablespoons tomato paste (purée)

500 g (1 lb 2 oz) skinless flake
2 onions, each cut into 8 chunks
2 small green or red capsicums
  (peppers), each deseeded and cut
  into 8 chunks
1 Lebanese (short) cucumber, peeled
  and diced
2 tablespoons chopped coriander
  (cilantro) leaves
lemon wedges, for serving

Fish substitution
  sea bream, snapper, grouper,
  orange roughy, sea bass

To make the marinde, mix half of the yoghurt, all of the other marinade ingredients and 1 teaspoon salt together in a shallow non-metallic dish that is long enough and deep enough to fit the skewers.

Cut the fish into approximately 24 bite-sized pieces. On each metal skewer, thread three pieces of fish and two chunks each of onion and capsicum, alternating them as you go. Turn the skewers in the dish containing the marinade so that all the fish and vegetables are well coated. Cover and leave to marinate for at least an hour in the fridge.

Preheat the barbecue or griller (broiler). Lift the skewers out of the marinade. Cook them on a barbecue flatplate or under the griller for about 5 minutes, or until the fish is firm and opaque.

Meanwhile, stir the cucumber and coriander into the remaining yoghurt. Serve the fish with the yoghurt and lemon wedges.

Serves 4

Barbecued squid with picada dressing

750 g (1 lb 10 oz) small squid,
  cleaned
rocket (arugula) leaves, for serving
crusty bread, for serving

Picada dressing
60 ml (¼ cup) extra virgin olive oil
3 tablespoons finely chopped flat-leaf
  (Italian) parsley
2 garlic cloves, crushed

fish substitution
  cuttlefish, octopus, prawns (shrimp),
  or even chunks of firm white fish
  fillet

To clean the squid, gently pull the tentacles away from the tube (the intestines should come away at the same time). Remove the intestines from the tentacles by cutting under the eyes, then remove the beak (if it remains in the centre of the tentacles) by using your fingers to push up the centre. Pull away the soft bone. Rub the tubes under cold running water and the skin should come away easily. Wash the tubes and tentacles and drain well. Place in a bowl, add ¼ teaspoon salt and mix well. Cover and refrigerate for about 30 minutes. Heat a lightly oiled barbecue flatplate.

For the picada dressing, whisk together the olive oil, parsley, garlic, ½ teaspoon freshly ground black pepper and some salt in a small jug or bowl.

Cook the squid in small batches on the barbecue for about 2–3 minutes, or until the tubes are white and are tender. Barbecue the squid tentacles, turning to brown them all over, for 1 minute, or until they curl up. Serve hot, drizzled with the picada dressing, with rocket leaves and crusty bread.

Serves 4

Salade Niçoise

3 large eggs
200 g (7 oz) green beans, trimmed
and cut in half

Dressing
100 ml (3¹/₂ fl oz) olive oil
50 ml (1³/₄ fl oz) red wine vinegar
1 teaspoon Dijon mustard
generous pinch of sugar
1 small garlic clove, crushed

1 Lebanese (short) cucumber, peeled
and cut into chunks
3 ripe Roma (plum) tomatoes, each
tomato cut into 8 wedges
1 small red onion, thinly sliced
225 g (8 oz) crisp lettuce, torn into
bite-sized pieces
1 small red capsicum (pepper),
thinly sliced
6 anchovy fillets in oil, drained and
cut in half lengthways
10 small black olives, pitted and
cut in half lengthways
1–2 tablespoons torn basil
175 g (6 oz) tin of tuna, preferably
in olive oil

Fish substitution
salmon, swordfish, marlin

Put the eggs in a saucepan of cold
water and bring to the boil. Reduce
the heat and simmer for 6–7 minutes.
Cool the hard-boiled eggs under cold
running water, peel and cut each egg
into four lengthways.

Bring a saucepan of water to the boil
and add the beans. Blanch for a
minute, then drain and refresh under
cold running water.

Make the dressing by whisking all the
dressing ingredients together.

Combine the beans, cucumber,
tomatoes, onion, lettuce, red
capsicum, anchovy fillets and olives
in a large bowl. Toss together to mix.
Add the basil, the tuna, breaking it
into large lumps, and the dressing
and gently toss again. Arrange the
eggs on the salad and serve. Serve
with a baguette.

Serves 4

Barbecued Asian-style seafood

500 g (1 lb 2 oz) prawns (shrimp),
  peeled and deveined, tails intact
300 g (10½ oz) scallop meat
500 g (1 lb 2 oz) baby squid, cleaned,
  tubes cut into quarters
500 g (1 lb 2 oz) baby octopus,
  cleaned
250 ml (1 cup) sweet chilli sauce
1 tablespoon fish sauce
2 tablespoons lime juice
60 ml (¼ cup) peanut oil
lime wedges, for serving

Put the prawns, scallops, squid and octopus in a shallow non-metallic bowl. In a separate bowl, combine the sweet chilli sauce, fish sauce, lime juice and 1 tablespoon of the peanut oil. Pour the mixture over the seafood and mix gently to coat. Allow to marinate for an hour. Drain the seafood well and reserve the marinade.

Heat the remaining oil on a barbecue flatplate. Cook the seafood, in batches if necessary, over high heat for 3–5 minutes, or until tender. Drizzle each batch with a little of the leftover marinade during cooking. Serve on a bed of steamed rice with wedges of lime.

Serves 6

Sweet and sour fish kebabs

750 g (1 lb 10 oz) thick ling fillets
225 g (8 oz) tin pineapple pieces
1 large red capsicum (pepper)
1 tablespoon soy sauce
1 1/2 tablespoons soft brown sugar
2 tablespoons white vinegar
2 tablespoons tomato sauce

Fish substitution
   cod, blue-eye, striped marlin

Soak 12 wooden skewers in cold water for 30 minutes. This is to ensure they don't burn during cooking. Meanwhile, cut the fish into 2.5 cm (1 inch) cubes. Drain the pineapple, reserving 2 tablespoons of liquid. Cut the capsicum into 2.5 cm (1 inch) pieces. Thread the capsicum, fish and pineapple alternately onto the skewers.

Place the kebabs in a shallow non-metallic dish. Combine the soy sauce, reserved pineapple juice, sugar, vinegar and tomato sauce in a small bowl. Mix well and pour over the kebabs. Cover and refrigerate for 2–3 hours.

Preheat the barbecue or chargrill pan. Cook the kebabs on a lightly greased barbecue, brushing frequently with the marinade, for 2–3 minutes each side, or until just cooked through. Serve immediately with a green salad.

Makes 12 skewers

Honey and lime prawn kebabs with salsa

32 prawns (shrimp), peeled and
  deveined, tails intact
3 tablespoons clear runny honey
1 small red chilli, deseeded and
  finely chopped
2 tablespoons olive oil
zest and juice of 2 limes
1 large garlic clove, crushed
2 cm (³/₄ inch) piece of fresh ginger,
  finely grated
1 tablespoon chopped coriander
  (cilantro) leaves

Salsa
2 tomatoes
1 small just-ripe mango, diced
¹/₂ small red onion, diced
1 small red chilli, deseeded and
  finely chopped
zest and juice of 1 lime
2 tablespoons chopped coriander
  (cilantro) leaves

Put the prawns in a non-metallic dish. Whisk the honey, chilli, olive oil, lime zest and juice, garlic, ginger and coriander together, then pour over the prawns. Toss well. Cover and marinate in the fridge for at least 3 hours, turning occasionally. Meanwhile, soak eight bamboo skewers in water for 30 minutes. This is to ensure they don't burn during cooking.

For the salsa, score a cross in the base of each tomato. Cover with boiling water for 30 seconds, then plunge into cold water. Peel the skin away from the cross. Dice the tomatoes, discarding the cores and saving any juice. In a bowl, mix the tomatoes and juice with the mango, red onion, chilli, lime zest and juice and coriander.

Preheat the griller (broiler) or a barbecue flatplate to high. Thread four prawns onto each skewer. Cook for 4 minutes, turning halfway through cooking. Baste regularly with the leftover marinade as they cook. The prawns will turn pink and be lightly browned on both sides. Serve the kebabs with the salsa and some rice.

Serves 4

Grilled red mullet with herb sauce

4 x 200 g (7 oz) red mullet
60 ml (¼ cup) lemon juice
60 ml (¼ cup) olive oil
parsley, for garnish
lemon wedges, for serving

Herb sauce
100 g (3½ oz) English spinach
60 ml (¼ cup) olive oil
1 tablespoon white wine vinegar
1 tablespoon chopped parsley
1 tablespoon chopped chives
1 tablespoon chopped chervil
1 tablespoon finely chopped capers
2 anchovy fillets, finely chopped
1 hard-boiled egg, finely chopped

Preheat the griddle or barbecue. Make a couple of deep slashes in the thickest part of each fish. Pat the fish dry and sprinkle inside and out with salt and pepper. Drizzle with a little lemon juice and olive oil and cook on the griddle or barbecue for 4–5 minutes each side, or until the fish flakes when tested with the tip of a knife. Baste with the lemon juice and oil during cooking.

To make the sauce, wash the spinach and put it in a large saucepan with just the water clinging to the leaves. Cover the pan and steam the spinach for 2 minutes, or until just wilted. Drain, cool and squeeze with your hands to get rid of the excess liquid. Finely chop. Mix with the oil, vinegar, herbs, capers, anchovy and egg in a food processor or mortar and pestle. Spoon the sauce onto a plate and place the fish on top to serve.

Serves 4

Barbecued sardines with pesto

12 sardines, scaled and butterflied
250 ml (1 cup) olive oil
1 tablespoon chopped rosemary
1 tablespoon chopped thyme
700 g (1 lb 9 oz) butternut pumpkin (squash)
2 small red onions

Pesto
30 g (1½ cups) flat-leaf (Italian) parsley
2 garlic cloves, peeled
40 g (¼ cup) macadamias
90 g (1 scant cup) grated Parmesan cheese
150 ml (5 fl oz) olive oil

Fish substitution
garfish, whiting, mackerel

Pat the sardines dry and place in a non-metallic container. Season the fish on both sides with salt and pepper. Mix the oil with the rosemary and thyme and drizzle over the fish. Leave to marinate for an hour or so, or until you are ready to cook. Heat a barbecue plate.

Meanwhile, slice the butternut pumpkin and cut into even-sized shapes measuring approximately 6 x 5 x 1 cm (2½ x 2 x ½ inches). Slice the onions in half widthways.

Make the pesto by putting all the ingredients in a food processor and whizzing to a paste. Alternatively, finely chop all the ingredients by hand and mix. Season to taste.

Barbecue the pumpkin, onion and fish for 2–3 minutes on each side, brushing regularly with the remaining herb oil. You will need a spatula to turn the pumpkin on the barbecue. Serve each person three sardines on a small bed of pumpkin slices with half a red onion and a generous spoonful of pesto on the side.

Serves 4

Octopus salad

650 g (1 lb 7 oz) baby octopus,
  cleaned
120 g (4½ oz) mixed salad leaves
lemon wedges, for serving

Dressing
2 tablespoons lemon juice
100 ml (3½ fl oz) olive oil
1 garlic clove, thinly sliced
1 tablespoon chopped mint
1 tablespoon chopped parsley
1 teaspoon Dijon mustard
pinch of cayenne pepper

Bring a large pan of water to the boil and add the octopus. Simmer for about 8–10 minutes, or until the octopus are tender to the point of a knife.

Meanwhile, make a dressing by mixing together the lemon juice, olive oil, garlic, mint, parsley, mustard and cayenne pepper with some salt and freshly ground black pepper.

Drain the octopus well and put in a bowl. Pour the dressing over the top and cool for a few minutes before transferring to the fridge. Chill for at least 3 hours before serving on a bed of salad leaves. Drizzle a little of the dressing over the top and serve with lemon wedges.

Serves 4

Beer-battered fish with crunchy chips

Batter
155 g (1 1/4 cups) plain (all-purpose)
  flour
375 ml (1 1/2 cups) beer

4 floury potatoes (e.g. desiree, bintje
  or King Edwards), cut into 1 cm
  (1/2 inch) wide chips (fries)
oil, for deep-frying
4 skinless firm white fish fillets, such
  as cod or haddock, patted dry
cornflour (cornstarch), for coating
lemon wedges, for serving

Fish substitution
  bream, coley, flake, flathead,
  pollack, snapper

Sift the flour into a large bowl and make a well in the centre. Gradually pour in the beer, whisking to make a smooth batter. Cover and set aside.

Soak the potatoes in cold water for 10 minutes. Drain and pat dry. Fill a deep-fat fryer or large saucepan one-third full of oil and heat to 160°C (315°F), or until a small cube of white bread browns in 30 seconds. Cook batches of chips for 4–5 minutes, or until lightly golden. Remove with a slotted spoon and drain on crumpled paper towels.

Dust the fish with cornflour, dip into the batter and shake off any excess. Deep-fry in batches for 5–7 minutes, or until golden and the fish is cooked through. Turn with tongs if necessary. You can check that the fish is cooked by cutting into the centre of one of the pieces—the flesh should be moist and opaque. Drain on crumpled paper towels. Keep warm in a low oven while you cook the chips again. Reheat the oil to 180°C (350°F), or until a cube of white bread browns in 15 seconds. Cook the chips for 1–2 minutes, in batches, until crisp and golden. Drain on crumpled paper towels. Serve the fish with lemon wedges and the chips.

Serves 4

Seafood pizza

Pizza dough

600 g (1 lb 5 oz) plain (all-purpose)
   flour, plus a little extra, for dusting
1 teaspoon dried yeast or 7 g (1/8 oz)
   fresh yeast
1 tablespoon olive oil, plus a little
   extra

350 g (12 oz) ripe tomatoes
2 tablespoons olive oil
1 large garlic clove, crushed
1/2 teaspoon sugar
pinch of chilli powder
1 tablespoon tomato paste (purée)
50 g (1 3/4 oz) squid, cleaned, cut into
   rings
165 g (5 3/4 oz) skinless cod fillets,
   cut into small chunks
110 g (4 oz) prawns (shrimp), peeled
   and deveined
50 g (1 3/4 oz) mussels, cooked and
   shells removed
8 anchovy fillets in oil, drained and
   patted dry
150 g (5 1/2 oz) mozzarella or Gruyère
   cheese, cut into small cubes
few sprigs of basil

Fish substitution
   haddock, sole

Mix 2 teaspoons of the flour in a large bowl with 60 ml (¼ cup) lukewarm water. Sprinkle the yeast over the top and stir to dissolve. Leave in a draught-free spot to activate. If the mixture does not bubble and foam in 5 minutes, it is dead—throw it away and start again.

Put the flour, the yeast mixture, 2 teaspoons salt, the olive oil and 200–250 ml (7–9 fl oz) water in a large bowl or in a food mixer with a dough hook. Mix together to form a dough, turn out onto a floured surface and knead for about 5 minutes. Put the dough back in the bowl and use your hands to smear the surface of the dough with a little extra oil to prevent it drying out. Cover with a tea towel and leave in a draught-free spot for about 2 hours, or until doubled in size.

Knock back the dough by punching it with your fist, then remove the dough from the bowl and divide into four portions. Dust with a little flour and roll into small balls. Place the balls on a tray or board dusted with a little flour and cover with a clean tea towel. Leave to rest for at least 30 minutes and up to 2 hours.

Meanwhile, make the topping for the pizza. Score a cross in the base of each tomato. Put in boiling water for 30 seconds, then plunge into cold water and peel the skin away from the cross. Roughly chop the tomatoes, discarding the cores. Heat the olive oil in a saucepan and, when hot, add the garlic. Cook for 30 seconds before adding the tomatoes, sugar, chilli powder and tomato paste. Bring the mixture to the boil, then reduce to a simmer and cook, uncovered, for 20 minutes, by which time the sauce will be reduced and thick. Season.

Once the dough is ready, preheat the oven to 230°C (450°F/Gas 8). Heavily dust the work surface with flour to prevent the dough from sticking, then use your hands to flatten out a dough ball into a circle. Finish off with a rolling pin to make a thin crust, about 2 mm (⅛ inch) thick, and transfer to a baking sheet or pizza tray. Repeat with the remaining balls.

Working quickly, spread the tomato mixture over the dough and scatter the seafood on top. Dot the cubes of cheese and sprigs of basil in between the fish. Season and bake for about 10 minutes, or until the base is golden and crisp and the topping is cooked.

Serves 4

Note: If you prefer, you can use ready-made pizza bases.

Fish plus

Spaghetti vongole

2 tablespoons olive oil
3 garlic cloves, crushed
2 pinches of chilli flakes
125 ml ($\frac{1}{2}$ cup) dry white wine
400 g (14 oz) tin chopped tomatoes
3 tablespoons finely chopped flat-leaf
(Italian) parsley
1 kg (2 lb 4 oz) clams (vongole),
cleaned
400 g (14 oz) spaghetti or linguine
$\frac{1}{2}$ teaspoon grated lemon zest
lemon wedges, for serving

Heat the oil in a large deep frying pan. Add the garlic and chilli and cook over low heat for 30 seconds. Add the white wine, tomatoes and 1 teaspoon of the parsley. Increase the heat and boil, stirring occasionally, for 8–10 minutes, or until the liquid is reduced by half.

Add the clams to the pan and cover with a lid. Increase the heat and cook for 3–5 minutes, or until the clams open, shaking the pan often. Remove the clams from the pan, discarding any that stay closed. Stir in the remaining parsley and season. Boil the sauce for 3–4 minutes until it is thick. Set half the clams aside and extract the meat from the rest.

Cook the pasta in a large saucepan of boiling salted water until *al dente*. Drain and stir through the sauce. Add the lemon zest, reserved clams and clam meat and toss well. Serve with the lemon wedges.

Serves 4

Prawn ravioli with basil butter

500 g (1 lb 2 oz) prawns (shrimp),
 peeled and deveined
1 tablespoon chopped chives
1 egg white, lightly beaten
330 ml (1 1/3 cups) cream
200 g (7 oz) packet gow gee
 wrappers (see Note)
1 egg, lightly beaten

Basil butter
125 g (4 1/2 oz) butter
1 garlic clove, crushed
3 tablespoons finely shredded basil
40 g (1/4 cup) pine nuts

Put the prawns in a food processor with the chives and egg white and process until smooth. Season with salt and pepper. Add the cream, being careful not to overprocess or the mixture will curdle. Transfer to a bowl, cover and chill for 30 minutes.

Put 2–3 teaspoons of the prawn mixture in the centre of the gow gee wrappers (you won't need them all). Brush the edges with beaten egg, then fold over and press together to form semicircles. Press the edges to seal. Add in batches to a large pan of boiling water and cook each batch for 4 minutes. Drain, taking care not to damage the ravioli, and divide among warm serving plates.

For the basil butter, melt the butter gently in a pan, add the garlic and stir until fragrant. Add the shredded basil, pine nuts and a little freshly ground black pepper, and cook until the butter turns a nutty brown colour. Drizzle the butter over the ravioli. Serve immediately.

Serves 8

Note: Buy the gow gee wrappers from Asian food stores—they are thin, round wrappers made from wheat flour and water.

Seafood risotto

1.75 litres (7 cups) fish stock
2 tablespoons olive oil
2 onions, finely chopped
2 garlic cloves, finely chopped
1 celery stalk, finely chopped
440 g (2 cups) risotto rice
8–10 black mussels, cleaned
150 g (5½ oz) blue-eye fillet, cubed
8 prawns (shrimp), peeled and
  deveined, tails intact
2 tablespoons chopped parsley
1 tablespoon chopped oregano
1 tablespoon chopped thyme

Fish substitution
  coley, ling, cod

Pour the stock into a saucepan and bring to the boil. Reduce the heat until just simmering, then cover.

Heat the olive oil in a large saucepan over medium heat. Add the onion, garlic and celery and cook for 2–3 minutes. Add 2 tablespoons water, cover with a lid and cook for 5 minutes, or until the vegetables soften. Add the rice and cook, stirring, over medium heat for 3–4 minutes, or until the rice grains are well coated.

Gradually add 125 ml (1/2 cup) of the hot stock to the rice, stirring over low heat with a wooden spoon, until all the stock has been absorbed. Repeat, adding 125 ml (1/2 cup) stock each time until only a small amount of stock is left and the rice is just tender— this should take about 20–25 minutes.

Meanwhile, bring 60 ml (1/4 cup) water to the boil in a saucepan. Add the mussels, cover with a lid and cook for about 4–5 minutes, shaking the pan occasionally, until the mussels have opened. Drain and discard any unopened ones. Set them aside until you're ready to add them to the risotto. Add the fish, prawns and the remaining hot stock to the rice and stir well. Cook for 5–10 minutes, or until the seafood is just cooked

and the rice is tender and creamy. Remove from the heat, add the mussels, cover and set aside for 5 minutes. Stir the parsley, oregano and thyme through the risotto, then season to taste with salt and freshly ground black pepper. Leave to rest for a couple of minutes, then serve.

Serves 4

Tagliatelle with prawns and cream

500 g (1 lb 2 oz) fresh tagliatelle or
   other long, flat pasta
60 g (2¼ oz) butter
6 spring onions (scallions), finely
   chopped
500 g (1 lb 2 oz) prawns (shrimp),
   peeled and deveined, tails intact
60 ml (¼ cup) brandy
310 ml (1¼ cups) thick (double/heavy)
   cream
1 tablespoon chopped thyme
15 g (½ cup) chopped flat-leaf
   (Italian) parsley

Cook the pasta in a large saucepan of boiling water until *al dente*. Drain well.

Meanwhile, melt the butter in a large heavy-based pan, add the spring onion and stir for 2 minutes. Add the prawns and stir for 2 minutes, or until they just start to change colour. Remove the prawns from the pan and set aside.

Splash in the brandy and boil for 2 minutes, or until the brandy is reduced by half. Stir in the cream, then add the thyme and half the parsley. Season with freshly ground black pepper. Simmer for 5 minutes, or until the sauce begins to thicken. Return the prawns to the sauce and cook for 2 minutes. Season well.

Toss the sauce through the pasta. If you prefer a thinner sauce, add a little hot water or milk. Sprinkle with the remaining parsley, then serve.

Serves 4

Seafood lasagne

1 tablespoon olive oil
30 g (1 oz) butter
1 onion, finely chopped
2 garlic cloves, crushed
400 g (14 oz) prawns (shrimp), peeled
  and deveined
500 g (1 lb 2 oz) skinless firm white
  fish fillets, cut into 2 cm (³/₄ inch)
  pieces
250 g (9 oz) scallops with roe,
  cleaned
750 g (1 lb 10 oz) bottled tomato
  pasta sauce
1 tablespoon tomato paste (purée)
1 teaspoon soft brown sugar
60 g (¹/₂ cup) grated Cheddar cheese
25 g (¹/₄ cup) grated Parmesan
  cheese
250 g (9 oz) fresh lasagne sheets

Cheese sauce
120 g (4¹/₂ oz) butter
85 g (²/₃ cup) plain (all-purpose) flour
1.5 litres (6 cups) milk
250 g (2 cups) grated Cheddar
  cheese
100 g (1 cup) grated Parmesan
  cheese

Fish substitution
  hake, snapper, flake, gemfish, ling

Preheat the oven to 180°C (350°F/ Gas 4). Lightly grease a 27 x 21 cm (10³/₄ x 8¹/₂ inch), 2.5 litre (10 cup) ovenproof dish.

Heat the oil and butter in a large saucepan. Add the onion and cook for 2–3 minutes, or until softened but not browned. Add the garlic and cook for 30 seconds, or until fragrant. Add the prawns and fish pieces and cook for 2 minutes before adding the scallops. Cook for a further minute. Stir in the pasta sauce, tomato paste and sugar and simmer for 5 minutes.

Combine the grated Cheddar and Parmesan cheeses in a bowl and set aside until needed for topping the lasagne.

For the cheese sauce, melt the butter over low heat in a saucepan, then stir in the flour and cook for 1 minute, or until the mixture is pale and foaming. Remove the pan from the heat and gradually stir in the milk. Return the pan to the heat and stir until the sauce boils and thickens. Reduce the heat, simmer for 2 minutes, then stir in the Cheddar cheese and Parmesan cheese. Season to taste with salt and freshly ground black pepper.

Line the ovenproof dish with a layer of lasagne sheets. Spoon one-third of the seafood sauce into the dish over the lasagne sheets. Top with one-third of the cheese sauce. Arrange another layer of lasagne sheets over the top. Repeat with the seafood sauce, cheese sauce and lasagne sheets until you have three layers, ending with a layer of cheese sauce. Sprinkle the top with the combined Cheddar and Parmesan cheeses. Bake the lasagne for 30 minutes, or until the top is golden. Leave for 10 minutes to firm up before slicing. Serve with a salad.

Serves 6

Mud crabs with rice noodles

1.5 kg (3 lb 5 oz) live mud crabs, each
  weighing approximately 250 g (9 oz)
150 g (5½ oz) dried thin rice noodles
5–6 tablespoons oil
2 red Asian shallots, thinly sliced
1 garlic clove, finely chopped
2 small red chillies, finely chopped
175 g (6 oz) bean sprouts, trimmed
175 g (6 oz) Chinese barbecued pork
  (char siu) or other cooked pork, cut
  into small pieces
60 ml (¼ cup) light soy sauce
2 tablespoons oyster sauce
2 tablespoons chopped coriander
  (cilantro) leaves

Freeze the crabs for 1 hour to immobilize them. Plunge them into boiling water for 2 minutes, then drain. Wash well with a stiff brush, then pat dry. Pull the apron back from underneath the crab and separate the shells. Remove the feathery gills and intestines. Twist off the claws. Using a cleaver or large knife, cut the crabs in half. Crack the claws using crab crackers or the back of a heavy knife. Soak the noodles in boiling water for 10 minutes, then drain.

Heat a wok, add 2 tablespoons oil and, when just smoking, add half of the crab. Stir for 1 minute, reduce the heat to medium and cover with a lid. Cook for 6 minutes, or until the crab shells turn bright red. Lift onto a plate, then repeat with the rest of the crab, adding 1 tablespoon oil, if necessary. Remove the meat from the shells and claws.

Heat the rest of the oil in the wok, then stir-fry the shallots, garlic and chilli for 5 minutes. Add the bean sprouts and pork and cook for 2 minutes. Add the soy sauce, oyster sauce, noodles, crab meat and coriander and stir until heated through. Season with salt, then serve.

Serves 4

Fusilli with tuna, capers and parsley

425 g (15 oz) tin tuna in spring
    water, drained
2 tablespoons olive oil
2 garlic cloves, finely chopped
2 small red chillies, finely chopped
3 tablespoons capers, rinsed and
    squeezed dry
30 g (1/2 cup) chopped parsley
60 ml (1/4 cup) lemon juice
375 g (13 oz) fusilli or other
    short pasta
125 ml (1/2 cup) hot chicken stock

Put the tuna in a bowl and flake it lightly with a fork. Combine the oil, garlic, chilli, capers, parsley and lemon juice in a small bowl. Pour the mixture over the tuna and mix lightly. Season well with salt and freshly ground black pepper.

Meanwhile, cook the pasta in a large pan of rapidly boiling salted water for 10 minutes, or until *al dente*. Drain. Toss the tuna mixture through the pasta, adding enough of the hot chicken stock to make it moist— you may not need it all.

Serves 4

Paella

125 ml (½ cup) white wine
1 small red onion, chopped
12–16 black mussels, cleaned
125 ml (½ cup) olive oil
1 small chicken breast fillet, cut into
  bite-sized pieces
1 streaky bacon rasher, finely
  chopped
4 garlic cloves, crushed
1 small red capsicum (pepper), finely
  chopped
½ small red onion, extra, finely
  chopped
1 ripe tomato, peeled and chopped
90 g (3¼ oz) chorizo, thinly sliced
pinch of cayenne pepper
200 g (1 cup) paella or short-grain
  rice
¼ teaspoon saffron threads
500 ml (2 cups) chicken stock, heated
80 g (½ cup) fresh or frozen peas
12 prawns (shrimp), peeled and
  deveined
100 g (3½ oz) squid, cleaned and cut
  into rings
100 g (3½ oz) skinless cod fillets,
  cut into bite-sized pieces
2 tablespoons chopped parsley

Fish substitution
  ling, mahi mahi, blue-eye, monkfish

Heat the wine and onion in a large saucepan. Add the mussels, cover with a lid and gently shake the pan for 4–5 minutes over high heat. After 3 minutes, start removing opened mussels from the pan and set aside. At the end of 5 minutes, discard any unopened mussels. Reserve the cooking liquid.

Heat half the oil in a large frying pan. Pat the chicken dry with paper towels, then cook the chicken for 5 minutes, or until golden brown. Remove from the pan and set aside. Heat the remaining oil in the pan, add the bacon, garlic, capsicum and extra red onion and cook for 5 minutes, or until the onion is softened but not browned. Add the tomato, chorizo and cayenne pepper. Season with salt and freshly ground black pepper. Stir in the reserved cooking liquid, then add the rice and mix well.

Soak the saffron threads in 125 ml (1/2 cup) of the hot stock, then add it, along with the remaining stock, to the rice and mix well. Bring slowly to the boil. Reduce the heat to low and simmer, uncovered, for 15 minutes, without stirring.

Put the peas, chicken, prawns, squid and fish on top of the rice. Using a wooden spoon, push pieces of the seafood into the rice, cover and cook over low heat for 10 minutes, or until the rice is tender and the seafood is cooked. Add the mussels for the last 5 minutes to heat through. If the rice is not quite cooked, add a little extra stock and cook for a few more minutes. Leave to rest for 5 minutes, then sprinkle with parsley and serve.

Serves 4–6

Kedgeree

350 g (12 oz) undyed smoked
  haddock
3 slices of lemon
1 bay leaf
300 ml (10½ fl oz) milk
175 g (6 oz) long-grain rice
60 g (2¼ oz) butter
1 small onion, finely chopped
2 teaspoons mild curry powder
1 tablespoon finely chopped parsley
3 eggs, hard-boiled, roughly chopped
170 ml (²/₃ cup) thick (double/heavy)
  cream

Fish substitution
  smoked cod fillets

Put the smoked haddock in a deep frying pan with the lemon and bay leaf, cover with milk and simmer for 6 minutes, or until cooked through. Remove the fish with a slotted spoon and break into large flakes. Discard any bones.

Put the rice in a saucepan along with 350 ml (12 fl oz) water, bring to the boil, cover and cook for 10 minutes, or until just cooked—there should be steam holes in the rice. Drain any excess water and fork through to fluff up the rice.

Melt the butter in a frying pan over medium heat. Add the onion and cook for 3 minutes, or until soft. Add the curry powder and cook for another 2 minutes. Add the rice and carefully stir through, cooking for 2–3 minutes, or until heated through. Add the fish, parsley, egg and cream and stir until heated through. Season well with pepper. Serve immediately with mango chutney.

Serves 4

Spaghetti marinara

Tomato sauce
2 tablespoons olive oil
1 onion, finely chopped
1 carrot, finely chopped
2 garlic cloves, crushed
400 g (14 oz) tin chopped tomatoes
125 ml (½ cup) white wine
1 teaspoon sugar

60 ml (¼ cup) white wine
60 ml (¼ cup) fish stock
1 garlic clove, crushed
12 black mussels, cleaned
375 g (13 oz) spaghetti
30 g (1 oz) butter
125 g (4½ oz) squid, cleaned and
  cut into rings
125 g (4½ oz) skinless cod fillet,
  cut into bite-sized pieces
200 g (7 oz) prawns (shrimp), peeled
  and deveined
10 g (⅓ cup) flat-leaf (Italian) parsley,
  chopped
200 g (7 oz) tin clams, drained

Fish substitution
  haddock, monkfish, plaice, or any
  firm white fish

To make the tomato sauce, heat the oil in a saucepan, then cook the onion and carrot over medium heat for 10 minutes, or until lightly browned. Add the garlic, tomato, wine and sugar, bring to the boil, then reduce the heat and gently simmer for 30 minutes, stirring occasionally.

Heat the wine, stock and garlic in a large saucepan. Add the mussels. Cover and shake the pan over high heat for 5 minutes. After 3 minutes, start removing any opened mussels and set them aside. After 5 minutes, discard any unopened mussels and reserve the cooking liquid.

Cook the spaghetti in a large saucepan of boiling salted water until *al dente*. Drain and keep warm.

Meanwhile, melt the butter in a frying pan and stir-fry the squid, cod and prawns in batches for 2 minutes, or until just cooked. Remove from the heat and add to the tomato sauce along with the reserved cooking liquid, mussels, parsley and clams. Gently heat through, then toss the sauce with the pasta and serve.

Serves 4

Fried rice

2 eggs, lightly beaten
2 tablespoons oil
1 onion, cut into wedges
250 g (9 oz) sliced leg ham,
  cut into thin strips
740 g (4 cups) cold, cooked
  long-grain rice (see Note)
40 g (¼ cup) frozen peas
2 tablespoons soy sauce
4 spring onions (scallions), cut on the
  diagonal into short lengths
250 g (9 oz) cooked small prawns
  (shrimp), peeled and deveined

Season the eggs with salt and freshly ground black pepper.

Heat 1 tablespoon of the oil in a wok or large frying pan and add the eggs, pulling the set egg towards the centre and tilting the pan to let the unset egg run to the edges. When almost set, break up into large pieces, to resemble scrambled eggs. Transfer to a plate and set aside.

Heat the remaining oil in the wok, swirling to coat the base and side. Add the onion and stir-fry over high heat until it starts to turn opaque. Add the ham and stir for 1 minute. Stir in the rice and peas and keep stirring for about 3 minutes, or until heated through. Add the egg, soy sauce, spring onion and prawns, and stir until heated through. Serve.

Serves 4

Note: Cook 275 g (1⅓ cups) rice a day in advance. Drain, cover and chill.

Mexican-style paella

1 large garlic clove, peeled
1 small onion, quartered
2 firm tomatoes
1 small red capsicum (pepper),
  quartered
60 ml (¼ cup) olive oil
50 g (1½ rashers) bacon, chopped
265 g (1⅓ cups) long-grain white rice
600 ml (21 fl oz) hot fish stock or
  water
2 tinned and drained, or fresh,
  poblano chillies, finely shredded
16 tiger prawns (shrimp), peeled and
  deveined, tails intact
250 g (9 oz) skinless snapper fillet,
  cut into bite-sized chunks
2 tablespoons chopped coriander
  (cilantro) leaves
1 lime, cut into four wedges

Fish substitution
  snook, gurnard, cod, halibut or
  other firm white fish, king prawns
  (shrimp)

Dry-fry the garlic, onion, tomatoes and capsicum in a large heavy-based frying pan over low heat for 45 minutes, or until browned all over, turning occasionally. Cool slightly. When cool enough to handle, peel the tomatoes and capsicum and roughly chop the flesh. Put in a food processor with the garlic and onion and blend to a purée.

Heat the oil in a deep sauté or frying pan. Add the bacon and cook until crisp. Tip in the rice and cook for a minute, stirring the grains to make sure they are all coated in oil.

Add the puréed vegetable mixture and cook for 3 minutes. Pour in the stock and 1 teaspoon salt. Bring to the boil and stir once. Reduce the heat to low and cover with a lid. Cook gently for 15 minutes. Add the chilli, prawns and fish to the pan and cook for another 5 minutes. Add a little hot water to the rice if it is becoming too dry. Season with salt if necessary. Sprinkle with coriander and serve with lime wedges.

Serves 4

Smoked salmon pasta

1 tablespoon olive oil
1 garlic clove, crushed
375 ml (1 ½ cups) cream
3 tablespoons chopped chives,
  plus extra, for serving
¼ teaspoon mustard powder
200 g (7 oz) smoked salmon, cut into
  strips
2 teaspoons lemon juice
500 g (1 lb 2 oz) fettucine or other
  long, flat pasta
3 tablespoons sun-dried tomatoes,
  chopped
2 tablespoons grated Parmesan
  cheese, for serving

Fish substitution
  smoked trout

Heat the oil in a frying pan, then add the garlic. Cook it briefly over low heat, being careful it doesn't burn. Add the cream, chives and mustard powder. Season to taste with salt and freshly ground black pepper, then bring to the boil. Reduce the heat and simmer, stirring often, until the sauce thickens. Add the strips of salmon and lemon juice and stir until heated through.

Meanwhile, add the fettucine to a large pan of rapidly boiling water and cook until *al dente*. Drain well and return to the same pan. Toss the sauce through the pasta, then divide among four bowls. Top with the tomato, Parmesan and extra chives.

Serves 4

Saffron prawn risotto

¹/₄ teaspoon saffron threads
60 ml (¹/₄ cup) olive oil
2 garlic cloves, crushed
3 tablespoons chopped parsley
500 g (1 lb 2 oz) prawns (shrimp),
    peeled and deveined, tails intact
60 ml (¹/₄ cup) dry sherry
60 ml (¹/₄ cup) white wine
1.5 litres (6 cups) fish stock
1 onion, chopped
440 g (2 cups) risotto rice

Soak the saffron threads in 60 ml
(¹/₄ cup) hot water.

Heat half the oil in a saucepan. Add
the garlic, parsley and prawns and
season with salt and pepper. Cook for
2 minutes, then add the sherry, wine
and saffron with the liquid. Remove
the prawns with a slotted spoon and
set aside. Simmer until the liquid has
reduced by half. Pour in the stock and
250 ml (1 cup) water, cover and keep
at a constant simmer.

In a separate large heavy-based
saucepan, heat the remaining oil.
Cook the onion for 3 minutes, or until
golden. Add the rice and stir over
medium heat for 3 minutes.

Add 125 ml (¹/₂ cup) stock to the rice
and stir constantly over low heat until
all the liquid has been absorbed. Add
125 ml (¹/₂ cup) stock and repeat the
process until all the stock has been
added and the rice is tender and
creamy—this will take 25–30 minutes.
Add the prawns and stir until heated
through. Season, then serve.

Serves 4

Asian prawn and noodle salad

Dressing
2 tablespoons grated fresh ginger
2 tablespoons soy sauce
2 tablespoons sesame oil
80 ml (⅓ cup) red wine vinegar
1 tablespoon sweet chilli sauce
2 garlic cloves, crushed
80 ml (⅓ cup) kecap manis

250 g (9 oz) dried instant egg noodles
500 g (1 lb 2 oz) cooked large prawns
   (shrimp), peeled and deveined, tails
   intact
5 spring onions (scallions), sliced on
   the diagonal
2 tablespoons chopped coriander
   (cilantro) leaves
1 red capsicum (pepper), diced
100 g (3½ oz) snow peas
   (mangetout), cut into halves
lime wedges, for serving

For the dressing, whisk together the fresh ginger, soy sauce, sesame oil, red wine vinegar, chilli sauce, garlic and kecap manis in a large bowl.

Cook the egg noodles in a large saucepan of boiling water for 2 minutes, or until tender, then drain thoroughly. Cool in a large bowl.

Add the dressing, prawns and remaining ingredients to the noodles and toss gently. Serve with lime wedges.

Serves 4

Phad Thai

10 tiger prawns (shrimp) or 20 small
   prawns (shrimp), peeled and
   deveined
200 g (7 oz) dried rice noodles
1 tablespoon dried shrimp
60 ml (¼ cup) oil
2 large eggs, lightly beaten
2 garlic cloves, crushed
1 small red chilli, finely chopped
2 tablespoons grated palm sugar or
   soft brown sugar
60 ml (¼ cup) lime juice
2 tablespoons fish sauce
50 g (⅓ cup) roughly chopped
   roasted peanuts
3 spring onions (scallions), sliced on
   the diagonal
75 g (2½ oz) bean sprouts, trimmed
3 tablespoons coriander (cilantro)
   leaves
lemon or lime wedges, for serving

Fish substitution
   any other raw prawns (shrimp),
   small scallops

If using tiger prawns, chop each one into three or four pieces, depending on their size.

Soak the rice noodles and dried shrimp in separate bowls of boiling water for 10 minutes. Drain.

Heat the oil in a wok until smoking. Add the beaten egg and leave to cook for 30 seconds, then stir to break into small pieces. Add the garlic, chilli and chopped tiger prawns and cook for 15 seconds, stirring all the time.

Add the sugar, lime juice and fish sauce and cook for 15 seconds, stirring and tossing in the wok. Tip in the noodles, 3 tablespoons of the peanuts and the dried shrimp. Toss together in the wok to heat through before adding the spring onions and bean sprouts. Cook for a further 30 seconds, then tip onto a serving plate and scatter the remaining peanuts and the coriander leaves over the top. Serve immediately with the lemon or lime wedges.

Serves 2

Risotto nero

1 litre (4 cups) fish stock
100 g (3½ oz) butter
1 red onion, finely chopped
2 squid, cleaned, heads discarded,
   tentacles set aside and bodies
   finely chopped
2 garlic cloves, crushed
350 g (12 oz) risotto rice
3 sachets of squid or cuttlefish ink,
   or the ink sacs from the squid
150 ml (5 fl oz) white wine
2 teaspoons olive oil

Pour the stock into a saucepan, bring to the boil, then keep at a low simmer.

Heat the butter in a large, wide heavy-based saucepan and cook the onion until softened but not browned. Increase the heat and add the chopped squid. Cook for 4 minutes, or until the squid turns opaque. Add the garlic and stir briefly. Add the rice and reduce the heat to low. Season and stir briefly to thoroughly coat the rice.

Squeeze out the ink from the sachets and add to the rice with the wine. Increase the heat and stir until all the liquid has been absorbed.

Stir in a ladleful of the simmering stock and cook over medium heat, stirring continuously. When the stock has been absorbed, stir in another ladleful. Continue like this for about 20 minutes, or until all the stock has been added and the rice is *al dente*. You may not need to use all the stock, or you may need a little extra— every risotto will be slightly different.

Heat the olive oil in a frying pan and fry the squid tentacles quickly, they should turn opaque and brown a little. Garnish the risotto with the tentacles and serve immediately.

Serves 6 as a starter

Pipis with spaghettini

1.5 kg (3 lb 5 oz) live pipis in the
    shell, cleaned
2 tablespoons olive oil
1 onion, finely chopped
2 large garlic cloves, crushed
150 g (5½ oz) button mushrooms,
    thinly sliced
100 ml (3½ fl oz) dry white wine
450 g (1 lb) ripe tomatoes, peeled
    and chopped
1 tablespoon tomato paste (purée)
pinch of sugar
500 g (1 lb 2 oz) spaghettini or other
    long, thin pasta
2 tablespoons chopped parsley

Fish substitution
    clams, cockles

Tip the pipis into a large saucepan, heat over medium heat and cover with a tight-fitting lid. Cook for 5 minutes. Discard any that have not opened. Strain the liquid into a bowl. Remove the pipis from their shells and set aside.

Meanwhile, heat the oil in a wide shallow saucepan or deep frying pan and add the onion and garlic. Cook over medium heat for 5 minutes, or until the onion is soft, then add the mushrooms and cook for a further 5 minutes, stirring now and then until they are cooked through. Pour the wine into the pan and allow to bubble for a couple of minutes. Add the tomatoes and any tomato juices, tomato paste, sugar and the cooking juices from the pipis. Bring to the boil, reduce the heat to medium and cook at a steady simmer, without a lid, for 20 minutes to allow the excess liquid to evaporate and the sauce to thicken. Place a large saucepan of salted water on to boil for the pasta.

Add the pipis to the sauce and gently heat through. Cook the pasta for 4–5 minutes, or until *al dente*, drain and return to the pan. Stir the parsley into the tomato sauce, season and pour over the pasta. Toss together and serve in large warm bowls.

Serves 4

Prawn jambalaya

1 kg (2 lb 4 oz) large prawns (shrimp),
  peeled and deveined, heads, shells
  and tails reserved
2 small onions, chopped
2 celery stalks, chopped
250 ml (1 cup) dry white wine
60 ml (¼ cup) oil
200 g (7 oz) chorizo or spicy sausage,
  chopped
1 red capsicum (pepper), chopped
400 g (14 oz) tin chopped tomatoes
½ teaspoon cayenne pepper
¼ teaspoon dried thyme
¼ teaspoon dried oregano
400 g (2 cups) long-grain rice

Put the prawn heads, shells and tails in a saucepan with half of the onion, half the celery, the wine and 1 litre (4 cups) water. Bring to the boil, then reduce the heat and simmer for 20 minutes. Strain through a fine sieve reserving the prawn stock.

Heat the oil in a large heavy-based frying pan and cook the sausage for 5 minutes, or until browned. Remove from the pan with a slotted spoon and set aside.

Add the remaining onion and celery, and the red capsicum to the pan and cook, stirring occasionally, for 5 minutes. Add the tomato, cayenne pepper, dried herbs and ½ teaspoon freshly ground black pepper and bring to the boil. Reduce the heat and simmer, covered, for 10 minutes. Return the sausage to the pan and add the rice and prawn stock. Bring back to the boil, reduce the heat and simmer, covered, for 25 minutes, or until almost all the liquid has been absorbed and the rice is tender. Add the prawns and stir through gently. Cover and cook for another 5 minutes, or until the prawns are pink and cooked through.

Serves 6

Flash fish

Chermoula snapper

Chermoula
125 ml (½ cup) olive oil
2 garlic cloves, crushed
¼ teaspoon cayenne pepper
1 teaspoon paprika
2 teaspoons ground cumin
2 tablespoons lemon juice
5 tablespoons finely chopped
   coriander (cilantro) leaves

1 kg (2 lb 4 oz) skinless snapper fillets
lemon wedges, for serving

Fish substitution
   bass, grey mullet, grouper, red
   emperor

To make the chermoula, mix the olive oil with the garlic, cayenne pepper, paprika, cumin, lemon juice, coriander and ¼ teaspoon salt. Place the fish fillets skin-side down in a large dish or on a tray. Brush the chermoula over the fish fillets, using up all the mixture, and leave them to marinate in the fridge for 1–2 hours, or overnight, if time permits.

Preheat a griller (broiler). Shake any loose bits of marinade off the fish and put the fillets on a foil-lined baking tray. Cook for 7–10 minutes, or until lightly golden on top and cooked through. Season and serve with lemon wedges.

Serves 4

Mahi mahi with lime sauce

4 x 200 g (7 oz) skinless mahi mahi
   fillets (see Note)
zest and juice of 2 limes
100 ml (3½ fl oz) dry white wine
1 large garlic clove, cut into slivers
200 g (7 oz) unsalted butter, chilled
2 tablespoons oil

Fish substitution
   sea bass, pompano, snapper,
   cod, John Dory

Put the fish fillets in a non-metallic
dish. Mix the lime zest and juice, wine
and garlic together and pour over
the fish. Turn the fish and leave to
marinate for 30 minutes, turning now
and then. Meanwhile, cut the butter
into cubes and return to the fridge.

Transfer the fish to a plate. Strain the
marinade through a sieve into a small
saucepan. Bring the marinade to
the boil and simmer until reduced to
2 tablespoons.

Meanwhile, heat the oil in a large
frying pan. When hot, add half of the
fish and cook for 3–4 minutes, turning
once, or until opaque and cooked
through. Repeat with the rest of the
fish and keep warm in a low oven.

Over a low heat, whisk the butter,
cube by cube, into the liquid left in the
saucepan, whisking thoroughly after
each addition. When half of the butter
has been incorporated, a few cubes
can be added at a time. Do not allow
the sauce to overheat. When all the
butter has been incorporated, season
to taste. Serve the sauce with the fish.

Serves 4

Fruits de mer with herb aïoli

Herb aïoli
4 egg yolks
4 garlic cloves, crushed
1 tablespoon chopped basil
4 tablespoons chopped flat-leaf
  (Italian) parsley
1 tablespoon lemon juice
200 ml (7 fl oz) olive oil

250 ml (1 cup) dry white wine
250 ml (1 cup) fish stock
pinch of saffron threads
1 bay leaf
4 black peppercorns
2 raw lobster tails, meat removed,
  shells reserved
12 black mussels, cleaned
250 g (9 oz) scallops, in their shells,
  cleaned
500 g (1 lb 2 oz) prawns (shrimp),
  peeled and deveined, tails intact
4 x 50 g (1¾ oz) skinless salmon
  fillets
lemon wedges, for serving

To make the herb aïoli, put the egg yolks, garlic, basil, parsley and lemon juice in a mortar and pestle or food processor and pound or mix until light and creamy. Add the oil, drop by drop from the tip of a teaspoon, pounding or processing constantly until the mixture begins to thicken, then add the oil in a very thin stream. (If you are using a food processor, pour in the oil in a thin stream with the motor running.)

Pour the wine and stock into a frying pan and add the saffron, bay leaf and peppercorns. Bring the liquid to a very slow simmer. Add the lobster meat and poach for 5 minutes, or until opaque, then remove from the pan with tongs or a slotted spoon, cover and keep warm. Poach the remaining seafood separately in batches. The mussels and scallops will take about 2 minutes to cook and open (discard any mussels that have not opened in this time). The prawns will take 3 minutes and should turn pink, and the salmon will take a little longer, depending on the thickness of the fillets.

Cut the lobster into thick medallions, trim and rinse the lobster shells and arrange the meat back in the shells. Put the scallops back on their shells. Arrange the seafood on a large platter, keeping each type together. If you like you can line the platter with rock salt to hold the shells steady. Scoop the aïoli into a small bowl and put it in the centre of the platter. Serve with lemon wedges.

Serves 4

Note: Provide finger bowls because this can get a bit messy.

Classic Venetian-style marinated sole

500 g (1 lb 2 oz) skinless sole fillets
50 g (heaped ⅓ cup) plain
  (all-purpose) flour
5–6 tablespoons olive oil
1 tablespoon raisins or sultanas
1 large onion, thinly sliced
150 ml (5 fl oz) red wine vinegar
100 ml (3½ fl oz) dry white wine
1 cinnamon stick
2 tablespoons pine nuts
pared zest of a small orange in strips
4 bay leaves

Fish substitution
  flounder, lemon sole, Dover sole,
  John Dory, brill, turbot

Lightly dust the fish fillets with the flour. Heat 3 tablespoons of the oil in a large frying pan and cook the fish in batches until lightly golden and crisp. Add another tablespoon of oil if necessary. Drain on crumpled paper towels. Arrange the fish in a single layer in a serving dish. Wipe out the frying pan.

Put the raisins in a cup, cover with warm water and leave to soak. Heat the remaining olive oil in the frying pan and add the onion. Reduce the temperature to low and cover with a lid. Gently stew the onion for 20–25 minutes, or until soft and translucent, stirring occasionally. Increase the heat and add the vinegar, wine and cinnamon stick. Boil for 3 minutes. Take the pan off the heat, drain the raisins and add to the onions along with the pine nuts, orange zest and a little salt and freshly ground black pepper.

Pour the marinade over the fish and tuck the bay leaves among the fillets. Cool, then cover and refrigerate for 24 hours. Serve at room temperature.

Serves 4

Sole Normande

500 ml (2 cups) dry white wine
12 oysters, shucked
12 prawns (shrimp), peeled and
  deveined
12 small button mushrooms or
  6 medium mushrooms, halved
4 skinless sole fillets
250 ml (1 cup) cream
1 truffle, thinly sliced
1 tablespoon chopped parsley

Pour the wine into a deep frying pan and bring to the boil. Add the oysters to the wine and poach for 2–3 minutes, then lift out with a slotted spoon, drain and keep warm. Poach the prawns in the wine for 3 minutes, or until pink and cooked through. Lift out and keep warm. Poach the mushrooms for 5 minutes, then lift out and keep warm. Add the sole fillets to the poaching liquid and cook for 5 minutes, or until the flesh is cooked through and opaque. Lift out onto a serving dish, cover and keep warm.

Pour the cream into the poaching liquid and bring to the boil. Boil until the sauce has reduced by half and thickened enough to coat the back of a spoon. Season with salt and freshly ground black pepper.

Put a sole fillet on each plate and scatter with the prawns, oysters and mushrooms, then pour the sauce over the top. Sprinkle with the sliced truffle and parsley and serve immediately.

Serves 4

Grilled Balmain bugs with foaming citrus butter

1 kg (2 lb 4 oz) Balmain bugs (see Note)
50 g (1³/₄ oz) butter
1 large garlic clove, crushed
1 tablespoon finely grated orange zest
1 tablespoon blood orange or regular orange juice
1 tablespoon lemon juice
1 tablespoon finely chopped chives
sourdough bread, for serving

Fish substitution
Moreton bay bugs, slipper lobsters, crayfish

Freeze the bugs for an hour to immobilize them, then plunge into boiling water for 2 minutes. Drain. Using a sharp knife or cleaver, cut each bug in half. Put the bugs on a large baking tray cut-side up and cook under a hot griller (broiler) for 3 minutes, then turn and cook for another 3 minutes, or until the flesh is white and opaque.

Melt the butter in a small saucepan and, when sizzling, add the garlic. Cook for 1 minute, stirring. Add the zest and juices to the garlic butter and bring to the boil again. Add the chives and season with salt and freshly ground black pepper.

Serve each person with some bugs and a small bowl of the hot foaming butter to dip the shellfish in. Serve with sourdough bread to mop up the citrus butter.

Serves 4

Note: Balmain bugs are named after a suburb in Australia located on Sydney harbour. They look like a small round flat lobster and have a sweet flavour, similar to crayfish or prawns (shrimp).

Teppan yaki with dipping sauces

Spring onion dipping sauce
1 spring onion (scallion), finely chopped
50 ml (1¾ fl oz) soy sauce
1 tablespoon mirin
1 tablespoon sugar

Sesame dipping sauce
2 tablespoons crushed white
  sesame seeds
2 teaspoons sugar
50 ml (1¾ fl oz) soy sauce
1 tablespoon mirin
1 teaspoon bonito-flavoured soup
  stock

oil, for greasing
4 spring onions (scallions), cut into
  6 cm (2½ inch) lengths
1 small red capsicum (pepper), cut
  into thin strips
1 small orange capsicum (pepper),
  cut into thin strips
8 small shiitake mushrooms, stalks
  trimmed and caps halved
400 g (14 oz) salmon fillet, cut into
  bite-sized cubes
16 prawns (shrimp), peeled and
  deveined, tails intact
400 g (14 oz) cleaned baby squid
lemon wedges, for serving

Fish substitution
  lobster, abalone, oysters

Prepare the dipping sauces first. For the spring onion sauce, mix the spring onion, soy sauce, mirin and sugar together, then pour into a dipping bowl. For the sesame dipping sauce, mix the crushed sesame seeds, sugar, soy sauce, mirin, stock and 1 tablespoon hot water together, then pour into a dipping bowl. Set both the bowls aside until needed.

Preheat a chargrill pan (griddle) or large frying pan until hot and grease with a little oil. (Alternatively, if you have an electric hotplate suitable for use on the dining table, you can cook in front of your guests.) Add half of the spring onion lengths, capsicum strips and mushrooms to the pan and cook for a couple of minutes, turning to ensure even cooking. When the vegetables are nearly cooked, push them to the edges of the pan or remove to a plate and keep warm in a low oven while you cook all the seafood.

Add half of the salmon cubes to the pan and cook for 1 minute before adding half of the prawns. Cook for 1 minute, then add the squid. Continue cooking for 2 minutes, or until the seafood is cooked, making sure you turn the seafood to cook all over. Add a little more oil as it is required.

Serve the seafood and vegetables together with the dipping sauces, the lemon wedges and some rice. Repeat the cooking order with the rest of the ingredients.

Serves 4

Note: Teppan yaki is usually eaten at specialized restaurants. The chefs work at grills around which the diners sit. The food is cooked in batches and served as it is cooked. When serving this at home, you can cook it all at once or serve in batches.

Greek-style calamari

Stuffing
1 tablespoon olive oil
2 spring onions (scallions), chopped
280 g (1½ cups) cold, cooked rice
  (see Note)
60 g (2¼ oz) pine nuts
75 g (½ cup) currants
2 tablespoons chopped parsley
2 teaspoons finely grated lemon zest
1 egg, lightly beaten

1 kg (2 lb 4 oz) squid (calamari) tubes,
  washed and patted dry

Sauce
4 large ripe tomatoes
1 tablespoon olive oil
1 onion, finely chopped
1 garlic clove, crushed
60 ml (¼ cup) good-quality red wine
1 tablespoon chopped fresh oregano

Preheat the oven to 160°C (315°F/ Gas 2–3). For the stuffing, mix the oil, spring onion, rice, pine nuts, currants, parsley and lemon zest in a bowl. Season well with salt and freshly ground black pepper. Add enough egg to moisten all the ingredients. Three-quarters fill each squid tube with the stuffing. Secure the ends with toothpicks. Put in a single layer in a casserole dish.

For the sauce, score a cross in the base of each tomato, put in a bowl of boiling water for 30 seconds, then plunge into cold water and peel the skin away from the cross. Chop the flesh. Heat the oil in a pan. Add the onion and garlic and cook over low heat for 2 minutes, or until the onion is soft. Add the tomato, wine and oregano and bring to the boil. Reduce the heat, cover and cook over low heat for 10 minutes.

Pour the hot sauce over the squid, cover and bake for 20 minutes, or until the squid is tender. Remove the toothpicks before cutting into thick slices for serving. Spoon the sauce over the calamari just before serving.

Serves 4–6

Note: You will need to cook 100 g (½ cup) rice for this recipe.

Salmon in nori with noodles

4 salmon cutlets, cut from the
   centre of the fish (ask your
   fishmonger)
1 sheet of nori (dried seaweed)
2 teaspoons oil
250 g (9 oz) somen noodles
2 spring onions (scallions),
   cut into long thin strips

Dressing
$1/2$–$3/4$ teaspoon wasabi paste
2 tablespoons rice vinegar
2 tablespoons mirin
1 tablespoon lime juice
2 teaspoons soft brown sugar
1 tablespoon oil
2 teaspoons soy sauce
2 teaspoons black sesame seeds,
   plus some extra, for garnish

Fish substitution
   ocean trout

Remove the skin and bones from the salmon, keeping the cutlets in one piece. Cut the nori into strips, the same width as the salmon, and wrap a strip tightly around each cutlet to form a neat circle. Seal the edges with a little water. Season with salt and freshly ground black pepper.

Heat the oil in a frying pan and cook the salmon for 2–3 minutes on each side, or until cooked to your liking (ideally, it should be a little pink in the centre).

While the salmon is cooking, prepare the noodles and dressing. Put the noodles in a large bowl, cover with boiling water and stand for 5 minutes, or until softened. Drain well. Combine the dressing ingredients in a jug and mix well.

Divide the noodles among serving plates, top with a salmon cutlet and drizzle with the dressing. Add the spring onion, then sprinkle with sesame seeds.

Serves 4

Note: Several of the ingredients in this recipe are Japanese, so you may need to source them from an Asian grocery store.

Fritto misto di mare

Garlic and anchovy sauce
125 ml (1/2 cup) extra virgin olive oil
2 garlic cloves, crushed
3 anchovy fillets, finely chopped
2 tablespoons finely chopped parsley
pinch of chilli flakes

Batter
210 g (1 2/3 cups) plain (all-purpose) flour
80 ml (1/3 cup) olive oil
1 large egg white

250 g (9 oz) baby squid, cleaned
12 large prawns (shrimp), peeled and deveined, tails intact
8 small octopus, cleaned
16 scallops, cleaned
12 fresh sardines, gutted and heads removed
250 g (9 oz) skinless ling fillets, cut into large cubes
oil, for deep-frying
lemon wedges, for serving

Fish substitution
cod, snapper

To make the sauce, warm the oil in a frying pan. Add the garlic, anchovies, parsley and chilli flakes. Cook over low heat for 1 minute, or until the garlic is soft but not brown. Serve warm or chilled.

To make the batter, sift the flour into a bowl and stir in 1/4 teaspoon salt. Mix in the oil with a wooden spoon, then gradually add 310 ml (1 1/4 cups) tepid water, changing to a whisk when the mixture becomes liquid. Continue whisking until the batter is smooth and thick. Cover and leave to stand for 20 minutes in the fridge. Whisk the egg white until stiff peaks form, then fold gently into the batter. Fill a deep frying pan one-third full of oil and heat to 190°C (375°F), or until a piece of white bread fries golden in 10 seconds.

Dry the seafood on paper towels. Working with one type of seafood at a time, dip it in batter. Shake off the excess batter, then lower into the oil, in batches if necessary. Be careful of the seafood exploding when it hits the oil. Deep-fry for 2–3 minutes, or until golden and crisp. Drain on crumpled paper towels, then keep warm in a low oven (but don't crowd it or it will go soggy). Sprinkle with salt and serve with the lemon wedges and the sauce.

Serves 4

Banana leaf steamed fish with fresh sambal

800 g (1 lb 12 oz) whole snapper, scaled, fins removed and gutted
2 lengths of banana leaf, each measuring approximately 60 x 40 cm (24 x 16 inches) (see Notes)
2 tablespoons unsalted peanuts
3 red Asian shallots, peeled
1 stem of lemon grass (white part only), cut into three pieces
small knob of fresh galangal, peeled
1 teaspoon grated palm sugar or soft brown sugar
60 ml (¼ cup) oil
½ teaspoon ground turmeric
1 tablespoon tamarind purée
1 tablespoon fish sauce
1 teaspoon sambal oelek or other chilli paste
60 ml (¼ cup) coconut milk
4 makrut (kaffir) lime leaves (see Notes)

Sambal
1 small mango, peeled, stone removed and cut into small dice
1 small red chilli, deseeded and finely chopped
2 tablespoons shredded fresh or dried coconut
1 tablespoon lime juice

Fish substitution
sea bass, coral trout

Score the fish with diagonal cuts on both sides.

If the banana leaf has been frozen it will be soft when defrosted, but if fresh and tough, blanch in boiling water for a minute to soften, then drain and refresh in cold water. Pat dry and place one of the pieces of leaf on top of the other so that they overlap by 10 cm (4 inches). Place the fish on top of the leaves. Alternatively, put the fish on a piece of foil.

Toast the peanuts in a low oven or in a saucepan on a low heat until golden. Allow to cool. Put the shallots, lemon grass, galangal and sugar in a food processor and whiz together to chop finely. Otherwise, chop and mix by hand. Heat the oil in a saucepan and when hot, add the chopped shallot mixture. Cook for 5 minutes, stirring, then add the turmeric, tamarind, fish sauce, sambal oelek and coconut milk and take off the heat. Allow to cool for 5 minutes, then spoon half of the mixture inside the cavity of the fish and the rest on the top.

Roughly chop the toasted peanuts, then scatter them over the fish with the lime leaves. Wrap the fish in the leaf or foil to make a parcel. Steam or barbecue for 25 minutes.

Meanwhile, make the sambal by mixing all the ingredients together, and then serve with the cooked fish.

Serves 2

Notes: If you don't have access to a banana tree, frozen banana leaves can often be found in the freezer section of Asian stores. Failing that, heavy-duty foil can be used instead.

Makrut (kaffir) lime leaves are quite unusual in that they have double leaves joined together at the tip—they resemble an elongated figure of eight. Most often the leaves have broken into halves by the time they reach the greengrocer.

Turbot en papillote with sorrel

25 g (1 oz) butter
1 small onion, finely chopped
125 ml (½ cup) dry white wine
170 ml (⅔ cup) fish stock
2 teaspoons oil, for greasing
1.5 kg (3 lb 5 oz) whole turbot, filleted into 4 pieces
2½ tablespoons crème fraîche
3 tablespoons chopped sorrel or basil leaves

Fish substitution
pompano, flounder, lemon sole, Dover sole

Melt the butter in a saucepan and add the onion. Cook for 10 minutes, or until softened but not browned, stirring now and then. Pour in the wine and stock and bring to the boil. Allow to boil for 10–15 minutes, or until reduced by half—you should end up with about 150 ml (5 fl oz).

Preheat the oven to 180°C (350°F/Gas 4). Cut four 30 cm (12 inch) diameter circles from baking paper. Lightly oil the circles, fold in half to make a crease along the middle and then unfold. Place a piece of fish on one half of each circle.

Once the sauce has reduced, add the crème fraîche. Stir, allow to bubble for 30 seconds, then remove from the heat. Season, stir in the sorrel, and then spoon a quarter of the sauce over the first piece of fish. Fold the empty half of the circle over the fish, fold the edges of the circle over twice and pinch together to seal. Repeat with the other pieces of turbot. As you make the parcels, lift them onto a large baking tray. Bake the fish for 15–20 minutes, depending on the thickness of the fish. Put the parcels on plates so they can be opened at the table.

Serves 4

Zarzuela

Sofrito base
1 tablespoon olive oil
2 onions, finely chopped
2 large tomatoes, peeled, deseeded
   and chopped
1 tablespoon tomato paste (purée)

Picada sauce
3 slices of white bread, crusts
   removed
1 tablespoon almonds, toasted
3 garlic cloves
1 tablespoon olive oil

1 raw lobster tail (about 400 g/14 oz)
750 g (1 lb 10 oz) skinless monkfish
   fillets
plain (all-purpose) flour, seasoned with
   salt and pepper
2–3 tablespoons olive oil
125 g (4½ oz) squid, cleaned and cut
   into rings
12 large prawns (shrimp)
125 ml (½ cup) dry white wine
12–15 black mussels, cleaned
125 ml (½ cup) brandy
3 tablespoons chopped parsley

Fish substitution
   cod, warehou, flake or any firm
   white fish

To make the sofrito base, heat the oil in a large flameproof casserole dish on the stovetop. Add the onion and stir for 5 minutes without browning. Add the tomato, tomato paste and 125 ml (1/2 cup) water and stir for 10 minutes. Stir in another 125 ml (1/2 cup) water, season and set the dish aside.

For the picada sauce, finely chop the bread, almonds and garlic in a food processor or by hand. With the motor running, or continuously stirring, gradually add the oil to form a paste.

Preheat the oven to 180°C (350°F/ Gas 4). Cut the lobster tail into rounds through the membrane that separates the shell segments, and then set aside. Cut the fish fillets into bite-sized pieces and lightly coat in flour. Heat the oil in a large frying pan and fry the fish in batches over medium heat for 2–3 minutes, or until cooked and golden brown all over. Transfer to the casserole dish with the sofrito.

Add a little oil to the pan if necessary, add the squid and cook, stirring, for 1–2 minutes. Remove and add to the fish. Cook the lobster and prawns for 2–3 minutes, or until just pink, then add to the casserole. Add the wine to the pan and bring to the boil. Reduce the heat, add the mussels, cover and steam for 4–5 minutes. Add to the fish, discarding any unopened mussels.

Pour the brandy into the pan, ignite and when the flames have died down, pour over the seafood. Mix well, cover and bake for 20 minutes. Stir in the picada sauce and cook for another 10 minutes, or until warmed through—do not overcook, or the seafood will toughen. Sprinkle with the parsley.

Serves 4–6

Crabs with spices, coriander and chillies

4 x 250 g (9 oz) small live crabs or
  2 x 500 g (1 lb 2 oz) crabs
125 ml (½ cup) oil
2 garlic cloves, very finely chopped
2 teaspoons finely grated fresh ginger
¼ teaspoon ground cumin
¼ teaspoon ground coriander
¼ teaspoon ground turmeric
¼ teaspoon cayenne pepper
1 tablespoon tamarind purée
1 teaspoon sugar
2 small red chillies, finely chopped
2 tablespoons chopped coriander
  (cilantro) leaves

Fish substitution
  large prawns (shrimp)

Freeze the crabs for 1 hour to immobilize them. Plunge them into boiling water for 2 minutes. Using a large heavy-bladed knife or cleaver, cut the crabs in half (quarters if you are using the large ones) and scrape out the spongey grey gills, then twist off and crack the claws. Turn the body over and pull off the apron pieces. Rinse under cold running water and pat dry.

Mix together half of the oil, the garlic, ginger, cumin, coriander, turmeric, cayenne pepper, tamarind, sugar, chillies and a generous pinch of salt. Heat the remaining oil in a large deep frying pan. When the oil is hot, add the spice mixture and stir over the heat for 30 seconds.

Add the crabs and cook, stirring for 2 minutes, making sure the spice mix gets rubbed into the cut edges of the crab. Add 2½ tablespoons water, cover and steam the crabs for a further 5–6 minutes, or until cooked. The crabs will turn pink or red when they are ready and the flesh will turn opaque. Drizzle a little of the liquid from the pan over the crabs, scatter with the coriander leaves and serve. Serve with crab crackers, picks, finger bowls and bread.

Serves 4

Stir-fried squid flowers with capsicum

400 g (14 oz) squid tubes
60 ml (1/4 cup) oil
2 tablespoons salted, fermented
  black beans, mashed
1 small onion, cut into small cubes
1 small green capsicum (pepper), cut
  into small cubes
3–4 small slices of peeled fresh ginger
1 spring onion (scallion), cut into short
  lengths
1 small red chilli, chopped
1 tablespoon Chinese rice wine
1/2 teaspoon roasted sesame oil

Open up the squid tube and scrub off any soft jelly-like substance, then score the inside of the flesh with a fine crisscross pattern, making sure you do not cut all the way through. Cut the squid into pieces that are about 3 x 5 cm (1 1/4 x 2 inches).

Blanch the squid in a saucepan of boiling water for 25–30 seconds— each piece will curl up and the crisscross pattern will open out, hence the name 'squid flower'. Remove and refresh in cold water, then drain and dry well.

Heat a wok over high heat, add the oil and heat until very hot. Stir-fry the black beans, onion, green capsicum, ginger, spring onion and chilli for 1 minute. Add the squid and rice wine, blend well and stir for 1 minute. Sprinkle with the sesame oil.

Serves 4 as part of a Chinese banquet or as a starter.

Scallops in black bean sauce

24 scallops, cleaned
2 tablespoons oil
1 tablespoon soy sauce
2 tablespoons Chinese rice wine
1 teaspoon sugar
1 garlic clove, finely chopped
1 spring onion (scallion), finely
  chopped
1/2 teaspoon finely grated fresh ginger
1 tablespoon salted fermented black
  beans, rinsed and drained (see
  Note)
1 teaspoon roasted sesame oil

Fish substitution
prawns (shrimp), crayfish or lobster,
baby squid

Begin by preparing the scallops. Heat 1 tablespoon of the oil in a wok and, when hot, add the scallops. Cook for 2 minutes, or until firm. Remove to a plate.

Mix together the soy sauce, rice wine and sugar in a cup with a tablespoon of water and set aside.

Add the remaining tablespoon of oil to the wok and heat until it is beginning to smoke. Add the garlic, spring onion and ginger. Cook for 30 seconds. Add the beans and the soy sauce mixture and bring to the boil. Return the scallops to the sauce with the sesame oil and allow to simmer for about 30 seconds. Serve immediately with rice and steamed Asian greens.

Serves 4

Note: Salted fermented black beans are fermented soya beans that have a distinct, salty flavour. They are used in the cooking of southern China.

Red mullet with baked eggplant

4 x 200 g (7 oz) red mullet, cleaned

Marinade
pinch of saffron threads
125 ml (½ cup) olive oil
2 tablespoons lemon juice
1 tablespoon pomegranate molasses
  (optional) (see Note)
1 small onion, grated
1 large garlic clove, crushed
1 tablespoon dried oregano
pinch of crushed dried chilli
1 teaspoon nigella seeds or
  ½ teaspoon cracked black pepper
1 teaspoon coriander seeds, slightly
  crushed
1 teaspoon cumin seeds

350 g (12 oz) eggplant (aubergine),
  cut into chunks
80 g (½ cup) pine nuts, lightly toasted
100 g (3½ oz) lamb's lettuce (corn
  salad) or baby English spinach
2 tablespoons roughly torn mint
1 tablespoon red wine vinegar
16 small black pitted olives

Fish substitution
  redfish

Lay the fish in a single layer in a shallow non-metallic dish. Infuse the saffron in a tablespoon of hot water for 10 minutes. Mix the saffron and its soaking liquid with half of the oil, a generous pinch of salt and the remaining marinade ingredients. Spread the marinade into the central cavity and over the skin of each of the fish. Cover and marinate in the fridge for 2 hours.

Transfer the fish to a large baking tray and scatter the eggplant around the fish. Brush the eggplant and fish all over with the remaining marinade. Cook both under a hot griller (broiler), turning now and then, for 20 minutes, or until the fish are cooked through.

Meanwhile, put the pine nuts, lettuce and mint in a bowl and toss well. Mix the remaining oil and the vinegar together and season. Dress the salad with the oil and vinegar mixture and divide among four plates. Scatter the olives and cooked eggplant over the salad leaves and place the red mullet on top. Drizzle a little of the cooking juices over each fish.

Serves 4

Note: Pomegranate molasses is a syrup with a sweet and sour taste.

Lobster Newburg

225 g (8 oz) raw lobster meat
50 g (1¾ oz) butter, plus extra for
    spreading on the toast
1 tablespoon sherry
1 tablespoon brandy
200 ml (7 fl oz) thick (double/heavy)
    cream
4 slices of bread
2 large egg yolks
pinch of cayenne pepper, plus a little
    extra, for serving

Fish substitution
prawns (shrimp), crab

Cut the lobster into small chunks. Melt the butter in a saucepan and, when hot, tip in the lobster. Cook for 3–4 minutes, or until the lobster is firm and tinged with brown. Mix the sherry and brandy together and pour over the lobster, light the alcohol by either tipping the pan towards the gas flame or with a match, and flambé the lobster (keep a saucepan lid nearby in case the flame gets out of hand). Using a slotted spoon, transfer the lobster to a plate and set aside. Add the cream to the pan and stir to heat.

Toast and butter the bread. Remove the crusts and cut each slice in two diagonally so you end up with eight triangles. Keep warm.

Lightly beat the egg yolks with a fork. Add 2 tablespoons of the warm cream mixture to the yolks and mix. Return to the sauce in the pan, whisk well, then put back on a low heat and stir for 3–4 minutes to thicken the sauce. The mixture must not overheat or boil or the eggs will scramble. Stir in the lobster and any juices on the plate. Season, add the cayenne pepper and serve on the triangles of hot buttered toast or, for a main meal, serve with boiled rice. Sprinkle with a little cayenne before serving.

Serves 4

Crawfish étouffée

2 tomatoes
100 ml (3½ fl oz) vegetable oil
50 g (1¾ oz) plain (all-purpose) flour
700 ml (24 fl oz) fish stock
2 large onions, chopped
1 small green capsicum (pepper),
  chopped
1 small red capsicum (pepper),
  chopped
75 g (2½ oz) celery stalks, chopped
1 large garlic clove, finely chopped
½ teaspoon paprika
¼ teaspoon cayenne pepper
1 teaspoon Worcestershire sauce
3 drops of Tabasco sauce
2 teaspoons chopped thyme
350 g (12 oz) crayfish (crawfish) tails,
  shells removed
3 spring onions (scallions), trimmed
  and chopped
2 tablespoons chopped parsley, plus
  a little extra, for garnish

Fish substitution
tiger prawns (shrimp), diced raw
lobster

Score a cross in the base of each tomato. Cover in boiling water for 30 seconds, then plunge into cold water. Drain and peel the skin away from the cross. Chop the tomatoes, discarding the cores. Set aside until needed.

Begin by making the dark brown roux. Pour the oil into a large heavy-based saucepan and heat through at a low temperature. Gradually add the flour, bit by bit, stirring in between each addition. You will end up with a thin roux. Continue to cook and stir the roux over a low heat until it turns a dark nut brown colour. This will take 30–40 minutes.

Towards the end of cooking the roux, pour the stock into another saucepan, bring it to the boil, then reduce to a gentle simmer.

Remove the saucepan containing the roux from the heat and immediately stir in the tomato, onion, capsicum, celery and garlic—the mixture will sizzle. Continue to stir the mixture for a couple of minutes or until it has cooled down. Add the paprika, cayenne pepper, Worcestershire sauce, Tabasco, thyme, $1\frac{1}{2}$ teaspoons salt and $\frac{1}{4}$ teaspoon freshly ground black pepper to the pan and stir to combine.

Return the mixture to a low heat and gradually add the stock, little by little, stirring in-between each addition. Once all the stock is incorporated, slowly bring to the boil, stirring, then leave on medium–low heat to simmer for 15 minutes. Give it a stir now and then to make sure it does not catch on the bottom of the pan.

Add the crawfish and cook gently for 5 minutes, or until it has turned opaque and is tinged with pink and orange. Stir in the spring onion and parsley and check the seasoning, adding more salt if necessary. Sprinkle with a little extra parsley and serve with rice.

Serves 4

Teriyaki salmon with soba noodles

12 dried shiitake mushrooms
1 teaspoon dashi granules
60 ml (¼ cup) Japanese soy sauce
2 tablespoons mirin
½ teaspoon caster (superfine) sugar
4 x 150 g (5½ oz) salmon cutlets
60 ml (¼ cup) teriyaki marinade
1 tablespoon honey
1 teaspoon sesame oil
250 g (9 oz) dried soba noodles
1 tablespoon vegetable oil
2 spring onions (scallions), sliced on the diagonal

Fish substitution
    mackerel

Soak the mushrooms in 500 ml (2 cups) boiling water for 10 minutes. Strain, reserving the soaking liquid. Pour the soaking liquid into a saucepan and add the dashi granules, soy sauce, mirin and caster sugar and bring to the boil. Simmer for 5 minutes.

Put the salmon, mushrooms, teriyaki marinade, honey and sesame oil into a non-metallic dish and allow to marinate for 15 minutes.

Bring a large saucepan of water to the boil and cook the noodles for 3–4 minutes, or until tender. Drain.

Heat the oil on a preheated barbecue. Take the salmon and mushrooms out of the marinade and cook over high heat for 3 minutes on each side, or until cooked but still slightly rare in the centre. Pour the reserved marinade over the fish during cooking.

To serve, divide the noodles among four serving bowls, pour over the broth from the mushrooms, then top with the salmon and mushrooms and sprinkle with spring onions.

Serves 4

Chilli crab

2 x 1 kg (2 lb 4 oz) fresh mud crabs
2 tablespoons oil
1 onion, chopped
4 garlic cloves, crushed
3 teaspoons grated fresh ginger
2–3 red chillies, finely chopped
400 g (14 oz) tin chopped tomatoes, puréed
1 tablespoon soy sauce
1 tablespoon soft brown sugar
2 teaspoons clear rice vinegar

Freeze the crabs for about 1 hour to immobilize them. Plunge into boiling water for 2 minutes. Wash well with a stiff brush, then pull the apron off from underneath the crab and separate the shells. Remove the feathery gills and intestines. Twist off the claws. Using a cleaver or a heavy-bladed knife, cut the body into quarters. Crack the claws with a good hit with the back of a cleaver.

Heat a wok until very hot, add the oil and swirl to coat the inside of the wok. Stir-fry the crab in batches for 2–3 minutes, or until bright red. Remove and set aside. Add the onion to the wok and cook for 3 minutes. Add the garlic, ginger and chillies, and cook for 1–2 minutes. Stir in the puréed tomato, soy sauce, sugar, vinegar and 125 ml (½ cup) water. Bring to the boil, then cook for 5 minutes, or until the sauce is slightly thickened.

Return the crab to the wok and toss to coat with the sauce. Simmer for 8 minutes, or until the crab is cooked, turning often.

Serves 4

Moroccan stuffed sardines

75 g (2½ oz) couscous
2 tablespoons olive oil
2 tablespoons chopped dried apricots
30 g (¼ cup) raisins
1 tablespoon flaked almonds, toasted
1 tablespoon chopped parsley
1 tablespoon chopped mint
grated zest of 1 orange
2 tablespoons freshly squeezed
    orange juice
1 teaspoon finely chopped preserved
    lemon
1 teaspoon ground cinnamon
½ teaspoon harissa
16 whole large sardines, butterflied
16 large fresh vine leaves or
    preserved vine leaves
400 g (14 oz) Greek-style yoghurt

Fish substitution
    small herring

Put the couscous in a bowl and add 1 tablespoon of the olive oil and 2½ tablespoons boiling water. Stir and leave for 10 minutes to allow the couscous to absorb the liquid.

Fluff the couscous with a fork and add the apricots, raisins, almonds, parsley, mint, orange zest and juice, preserved lemon, cinnamon, harissa and the second tablespoon of oil. Season with salt and pepper and mix.

Divide the stuffing between the sardines, folding the two fillets of each fish together to enclose the couscous mixture inside (save any extra couscous to serve with the sardines). Bring a pan of water to the boil and blanch the vine leaves for 30 seconds—you will need to do this in batches. Pat dry on crumpled paper towels. If you are using preserved vine leaves, rinse and dry them. Wrap a vine leaf around each sardine and secure it with a toothpick. Preheat a chargrill pan or barbecue flatplate. Cook the sardines for 6 minutes, turning them over halfway through. Serve each one with a dollop of yoghurt and any extra couscous.

Serves 4

Crispy fried fish with chilli and cucumber

500 g (1 lb 2 oz) whole pomfret,
  head intact, scaled and gutted
60 ml (¼ cup) oil
4 red Asian shallots or 1 small onion,
  thinly sliced
1 garlic clove, finely chopped
1 teaspoon grated fresh ginger
3 small red chillies, deseeded and
  finely chopped
2 tablespoons grated palm sugar or
  soft brown sugar
1 tablespoon tamarind purée
zest and juice of 1 lime
2 tablespoons fish sauce
1 large Lebanese (short) cucumber,
  peeled and cut into thin batons
oil, for deep-frying
1 tablespoon chopped coriander
  (cilantro) leaves

Fish substitution
  flounder, snapper, sea bass, bream

Score diagonal cuts on both sides of the fish.

Heat the oil in a wok or sauté pan. When the oil is just beginning to smoke, add the shallots and cook for 2 minutes, stirring, or until they are beginning to soften and colour. Add the garlic, ginger and chillies and cook for a further minute, or until lightly golden and crisp. Mix the sugar, tamarind, lime juice and fish sauce together and add to the sauce. Allow to bubble for 30 seconds, or until the sauce thickens slightly. Stir in the cucumber and take off the heat. Transfer the sauce to a small saucepan and leave to one side. Clean the wok or pan.

Fill the wok or pan 2.5 cm (1 inch) deep with oil and heat to 180°C (350°F), or until a cube of white bread dropped in the oil browns in 15 seconds. Lower the fish gently into the oil and cook for 4–5 minutes, or until golden and crisp. Make sure the skin does not stick to the wok and turn once during cooking. Spoon the hot oil over the fish as it cooks. Meanwhile, gently reheat the sauce. Drain the fish on paper towels. Drizzle the sauce over the fish, then sprinkle with lime zest and coriander.

Serves 2

Stir-fried fu-yung lobster

450 g (1 lb) lobster meat, cut into
  pieces
60 ml (¼ cup) Chinese rice wine
3 teaspoons finely chopped fresh
  ginger
12 egg whites
½ teaspoon cream of tartar
750 ml (3 cups) oil
125 ml (½ cup) chicken stock
¼ teaspoon white pepper
1 teaspoon roasted sesame oil
1 teaspoon cornflour (cornstarch)
3 tablespoons finely chopped spring
  onion (scallion)
2 tablespoons finely chopped spring
  onion (scallion) greens

Put the lobster meat in a bowl with
1 tablespoon of the rice wine,
1 teaspoon ginger and ½ teaspoon
salt, and toss lightly to coat. Beat the
egg whites and cream of tartar using
a balloon whisk or electric beater until
stiff. Fold the lobster into this mixture.

Heat a wok over high heat, add half
the oil and heat until very hot, then
add the remaining oil. Pour the lobster
mixture into the wok in batches—do
not stir the mixture, otherwise it will
scatter, but gently stir the oil from
the bottom of the wok so that the
'fu-yung' rise to the surface. Remove
each batch as soon as it is set, and
drain well. Remove the oil from the
wok, reserving 2 tablespoons.

Combine the stock, white pepper,
sesame oil, cornflour, the remaining
rice wine and 1 teaspoon of salt.

Reheat the wok over high heat, add
the reserved oil and heat until hot.
Stir-fry the spring onion and remaining
ginger over high heat for 10 seconds.
Add the stock mixture and cook,
stirring constantly to prevent lumps,
until thickened. Add the lobster
mixture and carefully toss it in the
sauce. Transfer to a platter, sprinkle
with the spring onion greens and serve.

Serves 6

Crab bisque

50 g (1¾ oz) butter
½ carrot, finely chopped
½ onion, finely chopped
1 celery stalk, finely chopped
1 bay leaf
2 sprigs of thyme
1 kg (2 lb 4 oz) live crabs, cleaned
    and claws detached
2 tablespoons tomato paste (purée)
2 tablespoons brandy
150 ml (5 fl oz) dry white wine
1 litre (4 cups) fish stock
60 g (2¼ oz) rice
60 ml (¼ cup) thick (double/heavy)
    cream
¼ teaspoon cayenne pepper

Heat the butter in a large saucepan. Add the vegetables, bay leaf and thyme and cook over medium heat for 3 minutes, without allowing the vegetables to colour. Add the crab claws, legs and bodies and cook for 5 minutes, or until the crab shells turn red. Add the tomato paste, brandy and white wine and simmer for 2 minutes, or until reduced by half.

Add the stock and 500 ml (2 cups) water and bring to the boil. Reduce the heat and simmer for 5 minutes. Remove the shells, leaving the crab meat in the stock, and reserve the claws to use as a garnish. Finely crush the shells in a mortar and pestle (or in a food processor with a little of the stock).

Return the crushed shells to the soup with the rice. Bring to the boil, reduce the heat, cover and simmer for about 20 minutes, or until the rice is soft.

Immediately strain the bisque into a clean saucepan through a fine sieve lined with damp muslin, pressing down firmly on the solids to extract all the liquid. Add the cream and season with salt and cayenne pepper, then gently reheat. Ladle into warmed soup bowls and garnish with the crab claws.

Serves 4

Salmon on skordalia with saffron–lime butter

Skordalia
500 g (1 lb 2 oz) potatoes, peeled and diced
3 garlic cloves, finely chopped
juice of 1 lime
100 ml (3½ fl oz) milk
150 ml (5 fl oz) virgin olive oil

Saffron–lime butter
100 g (3½ oz) butter
pinch of saffron threads
2 tablespoons lime juice

4 x 200 g (7 oz) salmon fillets
2 tablespoons oil
1 tablespoon lime zest
chervil leaves, for garnish

Fish substitution
  ocean trout

To make the skordalia, bring a large saucepan of water to the boil, add the potato and cook for 10 minutes, or until very soft. Drain thoroughly and mash until quite smooth. Stir the garlic, lime juice and milk into the potato, then gradually pour in the oil, mixing well with a wooden spoon.

To make the saffron–lime butter, melt the butter in a small saucepan, add the saffron and lime juice and cook until the butter turns a nutty brown colour.

Pat the salmon fillets dry. Heat the oil in a frying pan and cook the salmon, skin-side down, over high heat for 2–3 minutes on each side, or until the skin is crisp and golden. Serve the salmon on a bed of the skordalia, with the saffron–lime butter drizzled over the top. Garnish with lime zest and chervil leaves.

Serves 4

Barramundi steaks with shiitake mushrooms

2 tablespoons light soy sauce
2 tablespoons oil
2 tablespoons Chinese rice wine or
  dry sherry
pinch of sugar
zest and juice of 1 lemon
4 x 200 g (7 oz) barramundi steaks
  (see Notes)
1 teaspoon roasted sesame oil
150 g (5½ oz) shiitake mushrooms,
  sliced
2 spring onions (scallions), chopped

Fish substitution

snapper, swordfish, cod, salmon,
halibut steaks

Mix the soy sauce, oil, rice wine, sugar and lemon zest and juice together in a jug. Put the barramundi steaks in a shallow non-metallic ovenproof dish in which they fit snugly in a single layer. Pour the marinade over the fish steaks and turn them once so both sides are coated. Cover and refrigerate for at least 4 hours or overnight, turning occasionally. Return to room temperature. Preheat the oven to 180°C (350°F/Gas 4).

Heat the sesame oil in a frying pan and add the mushrooms. Cook, stirring, for 3–4 minutes, or until beginning to soften. Add the spring onion, stir and remove from the heat. Sprinkle the mushroom and onion mixture over the fish and bake, covered with a lid or foil, for 25–30 minutes, or until the fish is opaque and firm to the touch. Serve with egg noodles.

Serves 4

Notes: Barramundi, a highly valued fish, is found in the rivers, estuaries and sea of northern Australia. It has firm white flesh which matches well with the meaty texture of the shiitake mushrooms.

Shiitake are a dark brown mushroom, originally from Japan.

Sole meunière

4 Dover sole, gutted and dark skin
  removed
30 g (¼ cup) plain (all-purpose) flour
200 g (7 oz) clarified butter (see Note)
2 tablespoons lemon juice
4 tablespoons chopped parsley
lemon wedges, for serving

Fish substitution
  sole fillets

Pat the fish dry with paper towels, cut the fine bones and frill of skin away from around the edge of the fish, remove the heads if you prefer, and then dust lightly with the flour and season. Heat 150 g (5½ oz) of the butter in a frying pan large enough to fit all four fish, or use half the butter and cook the fish in two batches.

Put the fish in the pan, skin-side up, and cook for 4 minutes, or until golden (this will be the service side), turn over carefully and cook on the other side for another 4 minutes, or until the fish is cooked through (the flesh will feel firm). Lift the fish out onto warm plates and drizzle with the lemon juice and sprinkle with the parsley. Add the remaining butter to the pan and heat until it browns, but be careful not to overbrown it or the sauce will taste burnt. Pour over the fish (it will foam as it mixes with the lemon juice) and serve with lemon wedges and steamed greens.

Serves 4

Note: Clarified butter has a higher burning point than other butters. To clarify butter, heat a pack of butter until liquid. Leave until the white milk solids settle to the bottom. Use a spoon to skim off any foam, then strain off the golden liquid, leaving the white solids behind.

Poached Atlantic salmon

2.5 kg (5 lb 8 oz) Atlantic salmon,
  cleaned and scaled
3.75 litres (15 cups) court bouillon
  (see Basics)
½ cucumber, peeled
lemon wedges, for serving
mayonnaise, for serving

Fish substitution
  ocean trout, pacific salmon,
  sea bass

Put the whole fish in a fish kettle, pour in the court bouillon, then cover with a lid. Bring to the boil, reduce the heat and poach for about 15 minutes, or until the dorsal fin can be easily removed and the inside of the salmon looks cooked and opaque. Alternatively, you can use a baking dish big enough to hold the fish and bake the fish in a 180°C (350°F/ Gas 4) oven for about 25 minutes. Remove from the heat and let the fish cool in the liquid.

Remove the fish from the liquid and put on a work surface with the flatter side uppermost. Peel back the skin on this side, leaving the head and tail intact, and cut neatly around the head and tail. Turn the fish over and peel the other side. Make a cut horizontally down the centre of the salmon and gently separate the two pieces of fillet, then lift them off, being careful to keep them intact. Cut through the spine at the head and tail end and gently pull out the large bone. Pull out any bones which get left behind. Neatly replace the two pieces of fillet onto the lower fillet. Slice the cucumber into discs and then cut each one in half. Use these to decorate the salmon and hide the joins. Serve with lemon and mayonnaise.

Serves 8–10

Nigiri sushi

300 g (1⅓ cups) sushi rice
60 ml (¼ cup) rice vinegar
2 teaspoons caster (superfine) sugar
2 x 100 g (3½ oz) pieces of sashimi-
    grade tuna, cut into eight rectangles
    3 x 5 cm (1¼ x 2 inches), each
    5 mm (¼ inch) thick
wasabi paste
Japanese soy sauce, for serving
pickled ginger, for serving

Fish substitution
    halibut, trout, salmon

Wash the rice under cold running water. Put the rice into a saucepan with 250 ml (1 cup) cold water. Cover the pan and bring to the boil. Reduce the heat and simmer for 10 minutes.

Meanwhile, mix 2 tablespoons of the vinegar, the sugar and 1 teaspoon salt together. When the rice is cooked, remove from the heat and let it stand, covered, for 10 minutes. Transfer the rice to a bowl. Add the rice vinegar mixture, bit by bit, turning and folding the rice in the bowl using a wooden spoon or spatula. Continue to fold until the rice is cool. Cover the pan with a damp tea towel and set aside—do not refrigerate.

When you are ready to form the sushi, mix the remaining vinegar into 60 ml (¼ cup) water in a small bowl. Use the vinegar water to stop the rice sticking to your fingers. Using 1 tablespoon of rice, put the rice in the palm of one hand and use the fingers of the other hand to shape it into an oval shape. You should end up with 16 ovals. Hold each rice shape in your hand and, using a finger, spread a smear of wasabi paste in the middle. Top each with a piece of fish, moulding the fish onto the rice. Serve with soy sauce, extra wasabi and pickled ginger.

Serves 4

Lobster thermidor

1 cooked lobster
85 g (3 oz) butter
4 spring onions (scallions), finely
  chopped
1 1/2 tablespoons plain (all-purpose)
  flour
1/2 teaspoon mustard powder
2 tablespoons white wine or sherry
250 ml (1 cup) milk
60 ml (1/4 cup) cream
1 tablespoon chopped parsley
65 g (1/2 cup) grated Gruyère cheese
lemon wedges, for serving

Using a sharp knife, cut the lobster in half lengthways through the shell. Lift the meat from the tail and body. Remove the cream-coloured vein and soft body matter and discard. Cut the meat into 2 cm (3/4 inch) pieces, cover and refrigerate. Wash the head and shell halves, then drain and pat dry.

Heat 60 g (2 1/4 oz) of the butter in a frying pan, add the spring onion and stir for 2 minutes. Stir in the flour and mustard and cook for 1 minute, or until pale and foaming. Remove from the heat and gradually stir in the wine and milk. Return to the heat and stir constantly until the mixture boils and thickens. Reduce the heat and simmer for 1 minute. Stir in the cream, parsley and lobster meat, then season with salt and pepper. Stir over low heat until the lobster is heated through.

Spoon the mixture into the lobster shells, sprinkle with cheese and dot with the remaining butter. Place under a hot griller (broiler) and cook for 2 minutes, or until lightly browned. Serve with salad and some wedges of lemon.

Serves 2

Futomaki sushi

4 dried shiitake mushrooms
200 g (1 cup) sushi rice
1 tablespoon rice vinegar
2 tablespoons, plus two generous
    pinches, caster (superfine) sugar
1 tablespoon mirin
½ small carrot, cut in half
1 large egg
1 teaspoon sake
1 teaspoon oil
2 sheets of toasted nori seaweed,
    each measuring 20 x 18 cm
    (8 x 7 inches)
2 crabsticks (40 g/1½ oz) each, cut
    into strips
25 g (1 oz) pickled daikon, cut into
    strips
25 g (1 oz) cucumber, cut into strips
Japanese soy sauce, for serving
wasabi paste, for serving
pickled ginger, for serving

Place the mushrooms in a small saucepan and cover with 300 ml (10½ fl oz) boiling water. Place a saucer on top of the mushrooms to submerge them in the liquid, and leave to soak for 30 minutes.

Rinse the rice under cold running water. Put the rice into a saucepan and cover with 200 ml (7 fl oz) cold water. Cover the pan and bring the water to the boil. Reduce the heat and simmer for 10 minutes.

While the rice is cooking, mix together the vinegar, a pinch of the sugar and a generous pinch of salt. When the rice is cooked, remove the pan from the heat and let it stand, covered, for 10 minutes.

Transfer the rice to a bowl. Add the rice vinegar mixture, bit by bit, turning and folding the rice in the bowl using a wooden spoon or spatula. Continue to fold until the rice is cool. Cover the pan with a damp tea towel and leave to one side, but do not refrigerate.

Add the 2 tablespoons of sugar and the mirin to the mushrooms and stir. Add the carrots and bring the mixture to a simmer. Cook for 10 minutes and then drain. Discard the mushroom stalks and thinly slice the caps. Cut the carrot pieces into thin strips.

To make the omelette, gently mix together the egg, sake, the remaining pinch of sugar and a pinch of salt. Heat the oil in a small square or round frying pan. Add the egg mixture and cook until firm around the edges but still slightly soft in the middle. Roll the omelette and then tip it out of the pan and onto a bamboo mat. Roll the omelette in the mat and leave until cold, then slice into strips.

Place a sheet of nori on the mat, shiny-side down. Add half of the cooked rice, leaving a 2 cm (¾ inch) gap at the edge furthest away from you. Lay half of the filling ingredients on the rice in the following order: mushrooms, omelette, crabstick, daikon, carrot, cucumber. Starting with the end nearest to you, tightly roll the mat and the nori. Repeat this process with the other piece of seaweed and remaining ingredients.

Using a sharp knife, cut each roll into six slices. After cutting each slice, rinse the knife under cold running water to prevent sticking. Transfer to a serving plate and serve with soy sauce, wasabi and pickled ginger.

Serves 4

Cantonese-style steamed fish

750 g–1 kg (1 lb 10 oz–2 lb 4 oz) whole carp or barramundi, gutted through the gills, head and tail intact
2 tablespoons Chinese rice wine
1 ½ tablespoons soy sauce
1 teaspoon roasted sesame oil
4 tablespoons finely chopped fresh ginger
2 tablespoons oil
30 g (¼ cup) finely shredded spring onion (scallion)

fish substitution
  sea bass

Put the fish in a large non-metallic bowl. Add the rice wine, soy sauce, sesame oil and 1 tablespoon of the chopped ginger, and toss lightly to coat. Cover with plastic wrap and marinate in the fridge for 10 minutes.

Arrange the fish on a heatproof plate and put it in a steamer. Steam over simmering water in a covered wok for 5–8 minutes, or until the flesh feels flaky when the skin is pressed firmly. Remove from the steamer.

Heat a wok over high heat. Add the oil and heat until smoking hot. Sprinkle the steamed fish with the spring onion, the remaining ginger and ¼ teaspoon freshly ground black pepper, then slowly pour the hot oil over the fish. This will cause the skin to crisp and the garnish to cook. Serve with rice and vegetables.

Serves 6

Basics

Buying and storing seafood

Balmain bugs and other crustaceans

Bugs should have no discolouration or 'blackness', particularly at the joints. Bodies and claws should be fully intact. Bodies should be free of water or liquid and should be heavy in relation to their size.

When buying live bugs, they should be active and moving freely. Nippers and claws should be intact, not broken or loose. Store live bugs covered in a damp cloth in the salad compartment of the fridge for 1–2 days. To freeze, wrap the bugs in foil, place in an airtight freezer bag and freeze for up to 3 months.

Crabs

Buy live crabs from a reputable source as they are highly perishable. Look for lively crabs that feel heavy for their size. Crabs with worn barnacles and feet will not have just moulted—these crabs will have more meat. Mud crabs should be tied up until after they have been killed. Never buy a dead uncooked crab. Store live crabs covered in a damp cloth in a closed container in the coldest part of the fridge for 1–2 days. To freeze, wrap the crabs in foil, put in an airtight bag and freeze for up to 3 months.

Cooked crabs are also highly perishable, so buy with care. Make sure they smell fresh and are undamaged and their legs and feet are drawn into the body (if they were dead when cooked, the legs will be looser). Crab meat is also available frozen, tinned and in vacuum-sealed plastic bags.

Crayfish

Live should feel heavy and still be fairly lively. If they have not been purged (had their guts cleaned out) before sale, crayfish need to have their guts removed before eating. Cooked crayfish should have their tails curled tightly against their bodies and smell sweet and look fresh. Never buy dead uncooked crayfish.

Store live crayfish covered in a damp cloth in the salad compartment of the fridge for 1–2 days. To freeze, wrap the crayfish in foil, place in an airtight freezer bag and freeze for up to 3 months.

Fish fillets/cutlets

Fillets or cutlets should look moist and have no signs of discolouration. The fish on display should not be sitting in liquid. Fresh fish fillets should not look dried at the edges.

Fish fillets and cutlets can be stored for 1–2 days in a covered container in the coldest part of the fridge. Alternatively, they can be frozen in airtight bags for up to 3 months.

Lobster

When buying a live lobster, make sure it is lively and has its tail tucked under its body. The shell should be hard—a soft shell indicates it has just moulted and is not in peak condition. The shell should have no holes and the lobster should have all its limbs. When picking up a lobster, first make sure its claws are taped together, then pick it up just behind the head using your finger and thumb. Don't grasp it around its middle as it might close up on you suddenly.

Store live lobsters covered in a damp cloth in the salad compartment of the fridge for 1–2 days. To freeze, wrap the lobster in foil, place in an airtight freezer bag and freeze for up to 3 months.

Don't buy dead uncooked lobster as there is no way of telling what condition it is in and the meat deteriorates quickly. Lobster can also be bought already cooked—it should smell sweet and look fresh.

Mussels

Always buy mussels from a reputable source. Mussels are farmed extensively and these are safer to eat than wild ones as mussels are filter-feeders and many harbour toxins. Fresh mussels must be bought alive, as any that are dead may be toxic. The shells should be uncracked and closed, or should close when tapped on the bench.

Store live mussels covered in a damp cloth in the salad compartment of the fridge for 1–2 days.

Octopus and squid

The flesh should be firm and resilient and spring back when touched. The head, tentacles and body should be intact and not loose.

Fresh octopus and squid will last for 1 to 2 days in the fridge and for about 3 months in the freezer.

Oysters

Ideally, an oyster should be bought live, with the shell closed. In this state, it should be heavy and full of water. If buying an open oyster, prick the cilla (little hairs around the edge of the flesh): it should retract if the oyster is alive. Look for plump, glossy oysters that smell fresh. Unopened, oysters can be kept in the fridge for up to a week. If opened, store in their liquid and eat within 24 hours. Do not freeze.

Prawns (shrimp)

When buying raw prawns, avoid limp and soft ones that smell of ammonia or have any black spots or juices around the shell and head. Choose fully intact, firm and crisp prawns, with bright shells and a fresh sea scent. Most fishmongers also sell ready-cooked prawns, which takes all the bother out of the preparation.

Raw prawns will keep for 1–2 days in a covered container in the coldest part of the fridge. To freeze, place in a plastic container and cover with water—this forms a large ice block which insulates the prawns and prevents freezer burn. Freeze this way for up to 3 months. When required, thaw in the refrigerator overnight.

Scallops
Scallop flesh should be pale beige to light pink, moist and glossy with a fresh sea smell. The orange or pinky red roe is also edible. Scallops are sold either still enclosed in their shells or removed from the shell (shucked). Because they deteriorate rapidly once out of the water, they are usually sold shucked and should be refrigerated quickly and used within 1 day. They can also be bought frozen.

Whole fish
Fish should be considered seasonal to really get the most out of them, as supplies will vary according to spawning seasons and to fishing patterns. It is wise to buy the best fish that day, whatever it is, rather than an inferior fish just to fit a particular recipe.

Choose fish that have clear, bright and bulging eyes and avoid fish that have dull, sunken and cloudy eyes.

The skin and flesh should have a lustrous appearance and feel firm. If a fish can easily be bent so its mouth can kiss its tail, it is probably past its prime. Fish with scales should have a good even coverage and if patchy-looking are best avoided. Gills should be bright (from bright to dark red, depending on species). Some fish, such as salmon and trout, are covered in a clear slime (old slime is opaque). Oily fish deteriorate faster than white fish so be particularly vigilant when buying them.

Whole fish are best stored after they have been scaled and gutted (see page 391). Store in a covered container in the coldest part of the fridge for 2–3 days.

Preparing seafood

Butterflying sardines
Cut the head from the sardine, split open the belly with a sharp knife and remove the insides. Open out the sardine and place, skin-side up, on a chopping board. Press lightly, yet firmly, to open out. Turn over and pull out the backbone. Cut off at the tail end of the bones. Wash in salted water and dry on paper towels.

Cleaning clams
Wash the clams in several changes of cold water, leaving them for a few

minutes each time to remove any grit. Scrub the clams well. Drain well. Discard any broken clams, or open ones that don't close when tapped on the bench.

Cleaning mussels

Only use closed mussels or mussels that close when tapped on the bench. Scrub the mussels with a stiff brush and pull out the hairy beards. Discard any broken mussels, or open ones that don't close when tapped on the bench. Rinse well under cold running water.

Cleaning squid

To clean squid, gently pull the tentacles away from the tube—the intestines should come away at the same time. Remove the intestines from the tentacles by cutting under the eyes, then remove the beak by using your fingers to push up the centre. Pull away the soft bone. Rub the tubes under cold running water and the skin should come away easily. Wash the tubes and tentacles and drain well. The flaps can also be used. Use the body, flap and tentacles whole, or cut the body into wings.

Cutting round fish cutlets

Round fish (e.g. salmon, trout and bream) have a round body and eyes on either side of the head. Scale and gut your fish (see page 391). Use a large knife or, for a large fish, a cleaver, to slice cutlets. A cutlet (sometimes called a steak) is a thick slice through the body of the fish. Hold the fish firmly and cut through. Separate the whole fish into cutlets. If not using straight away, wrap individually and freeze.

Filleting flat fish

Flat fish (e.g. Dover sole) can yield four fillets, two from each side. Scale and gut your fish (see page 391). With a filleting knife, lay the fish dark skin-side up. Cut behind the head, then down the centre of the spine. Cut around the edge of each fillet and lift off using the knife to cut between the fillet and the bone. Turn the fish over and remove the other two fillets in the same way.

Filleting round fish

Round fish (e.g. salmon, trout and bream) yield two fillets, one from each side of the fish. Scale and gut your fish (see page 391). With a filleting knife, cut through the backbone and down the side of the head while using a sawing motion. To lift the fillet, start at the head end and run your knife blade between the flesh and the bones, keeping the knife close to the bone, until you reach the tail end. Turn the fish over and remove the other fillet in the same way.

Peeling and deveining prawns

Using your fingers, pull the head away from the body, then pull off the legs and peel the shell away from the body. If the prawns are to be served whole, they generally look better with the tails intact, otherwise they can be removed. Try to remove even the tiniest bits of shell so you don't crunch on them when eating. To remove the intestinal vein from prawns, start at the head end and use a skewer or a small finely pointed knife to remove the dark vein.

Preparing crabs

If the crabs are live, freeze them for 1 hour to immobilize them. Plunge them into boiling water for 2 minutes, then drain. Wash well with a stiff brush, then pat dry. Pull the apron back from underneath the crab and separate the shells. Remove the feathery gills and intestines. Twist off the claws. Using a cleaver or large knife, cut the crabs in half. Crack the claws using crab crackers or the back of a heavy knife.

Preparing octopus

Using a small knife, carefully cut between the head and tentacles of the octopus, just below the eyes. Grasp the body of the octopus and push the beak out and up through the centre of the tentacles with your finger. Cut the eyes from the head of the octopus by slicing a small round off, with a small sharp knife. Discard the eye section. To clean the octopus, carefully slit through one side, avoiding the ink sac, and scrape out any gut from inside. When you have slit the head open, rinse under running water to remove any remaining gut.

Preparing lobster, cooked

Grasp the head and body with two hands and twist them firmly in opposite directions, to release the tail. With scissors, cut down both sides of the shell on the underside, placing the scissors between the flesh and soft shell. Peel back the soft undershell to reveal the flesh. Gently pull out the flesh in one piece. Scrape the meat out of the claws with a lobster pick. Gently pull out the vein, starting at the head end, or remove when cutting the lobster into medallions or pieces.

Preparing lobster, live

Lobster bought live has the best flavour. The most humane way to kill lobster and other crustaceans is to put them in the freezer for 1 hour, then plunge in boiling water.

Cut into the membrane on the underside of the lobster, where the head and body join, to loosen. Twist or cut off to remove the tail. Cut down both sides of the shell on the underside, between the flesh and soft undershell using a pair of scissors. Peel back the soft undershell. Gently pull out the flesh in one piece. Pull out the vein from the back with your fingers, or when cutting.

Preparing scallops

If you are starting with scallops still enclosed in their shell, start by scrubbing clean the shells. For easy shucking, put it under a griller (broiler) for 1 minute to warm. Hold the scallop in a tea towel and, with a sharp knife, carefully prise open the shell. Lift off the top shell. Loosen the scallop from the shell.

With a small sharp knife, carefully slice off and discard any vein, membrane or hard white muscle from each scallop. The pinky red roe is edible but may be removed if you prefer.

Scaling and gutting fish

Fish need to be gutted fairly quickly as their digestive juices can break down and start to decompose their flesh. Preferably scale your fish outdoors, in a plastic bag or in the sink. Hold the fish firmly at the tail. Lifting it slightly, scrape against the direction of the scales with a fish scaler or sharp knife. Rinse well. Use a sharp knife to slit the belly, then remove the gut. Rinse under cold water, then pat dry with paper towel.

Shucking oysters

Wrap a tea towel around the unshucked oyster. Work an oyster shucker into the oyster and twist to break the hinge. Remove the top shell, slip the shucker between the oyster and the shell to release. Rinse both to remove grit. Replace the oyster.

Skinning a fish fillet

Depending on the recipe, you may or may not need to skin your fish. If the fish will be covered with a sauce, it will be easier to eat the fish with its skin removed. Remove the skin before cooking, or if cooking a whole fish, carefully peel it off after cooking. To skin a fillet, lay the fillet skin-side down on a board, with its tail towards you. Make a small cut through the flesh to the skin. Put the knife blade through the cut against the skin and slide or push the blade away from you. Hold onto the skin firmly. Carry on sliding the blade up to the head. You may need to move the blade from side to side as the fillet gets thicker.

Skinning Dover sole

Dover sole can have their skins removed whole. To do this, make a small cut at the tail end and loosen a piece of skin, then hold the fish down with one hand and the skin in the other and firmly pull it towards the head—it should peel off.

Cooking and serving seafood

Serving whole fish
Run a spoon or knife down the centre of the fish, then pull the fish from the bone. Lift out all the bones and cut off near the tail. Serve the fish in sections.

Testing that fish is cooked
Most fish is cooked when it loses its translucent appearance and turns opaque. When tested with a fork, the flesh starts to flake and separate from the bone. Some fish, such as tuna and Atlantic salmon, is best served while it is still rare in the centre. Don't overcook fish, take it off the heat as soon as it is 'just done'—the internal heat will finish the cooking process.

Testing that molluscs are cooked
Molluscs can be cooked briefly or eaten raw. The shells can be prised open—you may need to cut the muscle, or they can be steamed open.

Testing that prawns are cooked
When prawns are cooked, they should have turned pink and be curled.

Testing that seafood is cooked
Most seafood is cooked when it loses its translucent appearance and turns opaque. Don't overcook seafood or it will be dry, tough and rubbery.

Basic recipes

Court bouillon
Pour 2 litres (8 cups) dry white wine, 60 ml (¼ cup) white wine vinegar and 2.5 litres (10 cups) water into a large saucepan. Stud 2 onions with 5 cloves each and add to the pan along with 4 chopped carrots, 1 quartered lemon, 2 bay leaves, 4 sprigs of parsley and 1 teaspoon black peppercorns. Bring to the boil, reduce the heat and simmer for 30–35 minutes. Makes 3.75 litres (15 cups).

Fish stock
Put 2 kg (4 lb 8 oz) chopped clean fish trimmings, 1 roughly chopped celery stalk (including the leaves), 1 chopped onion, 1 unpeeled chopped carrot, 1 sliced leek, 1 bouquet garni, 12 black peppercorns and 2 litres (8 cups) water in a stockpot or large saucepan. Bring slowly to the boil and carefully skim off any froth that forms on the surface using a sieve or a ladle. Reduce the heat to low and simmer very gently for 20 minutes. Skim the scum from the surface regularly. Ladle the stock into a sieve, lined with damp muslin, sitting over a bowl. To keep the stock clear, do not press the solids, but simply allow the stock to strain undisturbed. Cool, then refrigerate for up to a week, or freeze. Makes 1.75 litres (7 cups).

Alternative names

anchovies *smig*

Atlantic salmon *salmon trout*

bonito *horse mackerel*

bream *porgy, silver or black bream*

coley *coalfish, saithe*

crab, blue *Atlantic blue crab, soft-shelled crab*

dabs *dab sole, flounder, garve, sand dab*

Dover sole *common sole, sole*

Dublin bay prawn *Langoustine, Norway lobster, scampi*

eel *European eel*

European carp *mirror, calico carp*

garfish *sea garfish, garpike, sea eel, needlefish*

grouper *hapuka, bass grouper*

John Dory *St Peter's fish, kuparu*

kingfish *yellowtail, southern yellowtail, southern yellowfish*

lemon sole *lemon dab, lemon fish*

ling *rock ling*

mahi mahi *dolphinfish, dorado*

monkfish *anglerfish, stargazer*

mullet, red *goatfish, barbounia, rouget*

mullet, sea *grey mullet*

orange roughy *red roughy, sea perch, deepsea perch*

parrotfish *tuskfish*

perch, ocean *coral perch*

pike *short fin pike, sea pike*

pilchards *adult sardines*

Pollack *green fish, lythe*

redfish *nannygai, red snapper*

sardine *bluebait pilchards (adult)*

scorpion fish *red rock cod*

shark *flake*

skate *ray*

snapper *cockney bream, red bream*

sole *see Dover sole*

squid *calamari*

trevally *skippy, jack*

trout, coral *leopard, blue spot trout*

trout, rainbow *river trout, steel head trout*

tuna, bluefin *southern bluefin*

warehou, blue *snotty-nose trevalla, black travalla, snotgall trevally*

whiting, sand *silver whiting*

Index

Index

Index

Published by Murdoch Books® a division of Murdoch Magazines Pty Ltd,
Pier 8/9, 23 Hickson Road, Millers Point NSW 2000

Editor: Zoë Harpham Editorial Director: Diana Hill
Designer: Michelle Cutler Creative Director: Marylouise Brammer
Photographers: Jared Fowler, Ian Hofstetter Stylists: Katy Holder, Cherise Koch
Food Preparation: Michelle Earl, Jo Glynn
Production: Monika Paratore
Recipes developed by the Murdoch Books Test Kitchen.

Chief Executive: Juliet Rogers
Publisher: Kay Scarlett

National Library of Australia Cataloguing-in-Publication Data: Fish food: great ideas
for cooking your catch. Includes index.
ISBN 1 74045 348 4. 1. Cookery (fish).
641.692

Printed by Tien Wah Press
PRINTED IN SINGAPORE

You may find cooking times vary depending on the oven you are using. For fan-forced ovens,
as a general rule, set the oven temperature to 20°C (40°F) lower than indicated in the recipe.
We have used 60 g (2¼ oz) eggs in all recipes.

IMPORTANT: Those who might be at risk from the effects of salmonella poisoning (the elderly, pregnant
women, young children and those suffering from immune deficiency diseases) should consult their doctor
with any concerns about eating raw eggs.

The Publisher thanks Steve Costi Seafoods for their assistance in the photography for this book.

Published by:
AUSTRALIA
Murdoch Books® Australia
Pier 8/9, 23 Hickson Road
Millers Point NSW 2000
Phone: (612) 4352 7000
Fax: (612) 4352 7026

UK
Murdoch Books Ltd UK
Erico House
6th Floor North
93–99 Upper Richmond Road
Putney London SW15 2TG
Phone: + 44 (0) 20 8785 5995
Fax: + 44 (0) 20 8785 5985